Managing Service Demand

A PRACTICAL GUIDE TO HELP REVENUE BODIES BETTER MEET TAXPAYERS' SERVICE EXPECTATIONS

OECD
BETTER POLICIES FOR BETTER LIVES

Please cite this publication as:
OECD (2013), *Managing Service Demand: A Practical Guide to Help Revenue Bodies Better Meet Taxpayers' Service Expectations*, OECD Publishing.
http://dx.doi.org/10.1787/9789264200821-en

ISBN 978-92-64-20076-0 (print)
ISBN 978-92-64-20082-1 (PDF)

Corrigenda to OECD publications may be found on line at: *www.oecd.org/publishing/corrigenda*.

Foreword

As a result of current global economic conditions, many revenue bodies around the world have been required to identify opportunities to reduce the costs of their administration as part of broader public sector cost-cutting efforts. Revenue bodies seek to find ways of achieving this objective whilst maintaining high standards of service delivery to the community.

At its 2012 meeting in Buenos Aires, the Forum on Tax Administration (FTA) issued the study Working smarter in revenue administration – Using demand management strategies to meet service delivery goals, which was conducted by its Taxpayer Services Sub-Group. The study identified service demand management processes that revenue bodies had in place that enabled a better understanding of drivers of service demand. It also identified those processes that reduced demand or enabled demand to be shifted to more cost-efficient channels.

The study resulted in the compilation of this guide to assist revenue bodies manage service demand efficiently and effectively. It sets out practical steps in the form of a step-by-step framework to support revenue bodies in their efforts to better identify, analyse and address the causes of service demand. It also sets out a possible 'model' for governance arrangements based on leading revenue body practice.

This guide was prepared by the Australian Taxation Office (ATO), supported by a task group of 12 countries (Canada, Chile, Finland, Ireland, Japan, Korea, Mexico, New Zealand, Norway, Switzerland, Turkey and United Kingdom) and the FTA Secretariat.

The Forum on Tax Administration and the Taxpayer Services Sub-Group

The Forum on Tax Administration (FTA) was created by the Committee on Fiscal Affairs in July 2002. Since then the FTA has grown to become a unique forum on tax administration for the heads of revenue bodies and their teams from OECD and selected non-OECD countries. The work programme of the Forum is decided and overseen by a Bureau comprised of commissioners from 12 revenue bodies.

The FTA vision is to create a forum through which tax administrators can identify, discuss and influence relevant global trends and develop new ideas to enhance tax administration around the world. This vision is underpinned by the FTA's key aim which is to help revenue bodies increase the efficiency, effectiveness and fairness of tax administration and reduce the costs of compliance.

The FTA is supported by a number of specialist sub-groups and networks to help carry out its mandate: The Taxpayer Services Sub-group, the SME Compliance Sub-group, the Large Business Network, and the High Net Worth Individuals Network, and the Offshore Compliance Network.

The work of the Taxpayer Services Sub-group focusses on sharing member experiences and knowledge of approaches to taxpayer service delivery, in particular through the use of modern technology. Discussions and presentations at its annual meetings, often including external speakers, along with related surveys, studies and reports have all served to provide a valuable means for keeping tax administrations abreast of emerging issues and country approaches to making more effective use of modern technology for service delivery purposes.

More information on the FTA, including details on products and publications, can be found at its dedicated website: *www.oecd.org/tax/fta*

Table of contents

Figures

Tables

Executive summary

Revenue bodies have limited resources and face difficult choices in deciding how many resources they can devote to critical areas of work such as service delivery, given all of their priorities. The challenge is even greater where targets for overall resource reduction must be met and/ or there is an acknowledged need to improve the quality of the services delivered.

The FTA's 2012 report *Working smarter in revenue administration – Using demand management strategies to meet service delivery goals*, which sought to identify the service demand management processes that revenue bodies had in place and what steps they took to understand the root causes of service demand, highlighted a number of imperatives for further attention by most revenue bodies:

- many revenue bodies were continuing to experience high demand on their more expensive in-person and inbound call channels;
- most revenue bodies were measuring demand through a variety of methodologies and technologies; however, these methodologies were typically costly, time-consuming, labour intensive and, most importantly, not effective for determining the root causes of demand;
- internal revenue body governance processes for managing service demand were, for the most part, not sufficiently comprehensive, evidence-based, and systematic and therefore not particularly effective in eliminating service demand or shifting it to less expensive service channels.

As a consequence, the FTA Bureau decided that further work should be undertaken to provide practical guidance for revenue bodies on how such shortcomings might be addressed.

This note provides guidance on a whole-of-revenue body approach for managing service demand effectively. It sets out a possible 'model' for governance arrangements based on leading revenue body practice – in this case the Australian Taxation Office – that has been examined and is supported by the FTA's Taxpayer Services Sub-group. It also sets out practical steps in the form of a step-by-step framework to support revenue bodies in their efforts to better identify, analyse and address the causes of service demand.

The guide has been designed to support all revenue bodies, from those that are in the early stages of developing comprehensive service delivery programmes to those with mature programmes in place. While it focuses on the revenue body's role in tax administration it acknowledges that some revenue bodies have a broader set of responsibilities, for example, in the administration of some social policies. This guide has not explored how such roles should integrate at a broader demand management level and revenue bodies will need to assess this issue, if relevant, having regard to their individual circumstances.

Application of the guide should be considered in conjunction with individual revenue bodies' service delivery programmes and their resourcing strategies.

Chapter 1

Introduction

In the aftermath of the global financial crisis many revenue bodies around the world have been required to identify opportunities to reduce the costs of their administration as part of broader public sector cost-cutting efforts. At the same time, countries have generally demanded that their agencies, including revenue bodies, remain responsive to community expectations around the need to maintain high standards of service delivery.

During 2011 the Forum on Tax Administration (FTA), via its Taxpayer Services Sub-Group (TSG), conducted a study entitled *Working smarter in revenue administration – Using demand management strategies to meet service delivery goals*. The study aimed to identify the service demand management processes that revenue bodies had in place and what steps they took to understand the root causes of service demand and how that knowledge was applied to either reduce demand or shift it to more cost-efficient channels. Among other things, the study found that:

- despite having implemented multi-channel service models and setting service objectives to shift taxpayers to self-service and the online channel, many revenue bodies were continuing to experience high demand on their more expensive in-person and inbound call channels;
- most revenue bodies were measuring demand through a variety of methodologies and technologies such as manual processes, call centre and workload control systems and databases that provide useful information on volumes, trends and demand topics; however, these methodologies were typically costly, time-consuming, labour intensive and, most importantly, not effective for determining the root causes of demand;
- generally speaking, internal revenue body governance processes for managing service demand were immature – fragmented, incomplete, and/or lacking co-ordination.

The findings and recommendations of the study were subsequently discussed by the FTA's Bureau in early 2012, as a result of which it was decided that there would be value in developing a practical guide on an end-to-end process for managing service demand. The Australian Taxation Office agreed to take the lead in developing a practical guide, working in close collaboration with TSG delegates.

Methodology

The guide was prepared by the Australian Taxation Office (ATO), supported by a task group of 12 countries (Canada, Chile, Finland, Ireland, Japan, Korea, Mexico, New Zealand, Norway, Switzerland, Turkey, and United Kingdom) and the OECD Secretariat.

While the guide draws on a governance model and process framework developed by the ATO for its own purposes it has been "generalised" to have broad international application. It is also supported by a set of case studies provided by participating countries to demonstrate revenue body approaches and experiences to particular aspects of managing service demand.

An early version of the draft guide was discussed in detail with members of the FTA Taxpayer Services Sub-group in September 2012 and the feedback given enabled further refinement of the draft guide.

Chapter 2

Managing service demand

This chapter sets out elements of the broader environmental context that should influence a revenue body's plan for managing service demand to achieve improved performance.

The imperatives for effective management of service demand

Tax systems generally rely on the premise that the majority of taxpayers do comply with tax laws and will do so voluntarily if it is made as easy as possible to do so and they are supported when needed.

In an ideal world, all taxpayers would fully understand their tax obligations, meet the requirements of the law with minimal assistance, and be satisfied with the level of service and treatment provided by the revenue body. In reality, of course, this is not the case. Viewed from the perspective of citizens and businesses, there are a range of issues that can drive the need for assistance. Tax laws are often complex and compliance requirements can be quite demanding. A revenue body may have the additional responsibility for administering non-tax policies which bring their own complexities around understanding eligibility for benefits and services. Information to support completion of forms and transactions may not be easy to understand or the website may be difficult to navigate or locate relevant content. The challenging economic environment can impact the ability for taxpayers to pay their tax debts and a revenue body may not be able to meet community expectations for timeliness of service. The design and implementation of major tax policy changes, in short timeframes, can also present difficulties for citizens and businesses.

Practical difficulties of the kind outlined create a demand for revenue bodies' services in an environment where there are community expectations that good standards of service will be provided by government agencies whenever and wherever they are needed. For its part, a revenue body is challenged to allocate its limited resources across all of its responsibilities in order to optimise its performance in an overall sense.

Traditionally, interactions between taxpayers and revenue bodies were made face-to-face (often supported by a large network of offices to facilitate personal inquiries), by phone enquiries to distributed enquiry services and by written correspondence. However, particularly over the last decade or so, major technological advances and other developments have led to new opportunities – termed 'channels' in a service delivery context – becoming available for delivering services to taxpayers. The main developments have been the emergence of electronic channels – the Internet (both for static and interactive services delivery) – and the provision of dedicated phone centre contact operations supported by sophisticated telephony equipment. These new channels have increased the mix of channels available for service delivery and opened up new opportunities for revenue bodies to improve their performance.

In the environment outlined, revenue bodies attempting to satisfy taxpayers' service demands inevitably will be required to make a variety of trade-offs and choices in their planning and delivery of services to taxpayers. These challenges will be intensified where there are additional objectives to be met (for example, mandates to achieve significant reductions in administrative expenditures, improvements in the level of community satisfaction with the services delivery, and/or to successfully implement a major new government policy).

In managing demand pressures, a revenue agency needs to consider:

- that demand will generally outstrip supply;
- that increasing assets that deliver services will increase both the capital and operating costs of a revenue body;
- that increasing assets and services can generate and foster demand;
- that the 'root cause' and drivers for services is something the revenue body may not always be able to control;
- that there may be a need to encourage and promote greater use of some services to mitigate a particular revenue risk;
- that legislative and policy context constraints and the importance of good design to deliver services.

What is demand management?

Successful demand management can include:

- providing effective service outcomes to meet identified community needs;
- assessing if the need is changing;
- continually improving the services provided to the community and the way that the revenue body delivers them;
- responding appropriately and within the available resources, and
- driving demand to preferred channels.

In the context of revenue bodies providing services to the community, demand management involves:

- analysing and understanding why the community seeks the revenue body's services – understanding the 'trigger events';
- understanding which services provide a value to the community. It is also about understanding the cost of delivering those services – ensuring effective use of the revenue body's resources and eliminating the need for contact at all where possible;
- designing with 'channel' in mind – *i.e.* increase electronic, reduce paper;
- considering the client experience while maintaining a focus on the compliance outcomes for government;

- being clear about service levels and expectations within the community, which may include considering changes to service standards to increase response times for less preferred channels;
- increasing taxpayers' knowledge about the revenue body's services and preferred methods of interaction, and
- recognising the value and role that an intermediary, such as a tax professional or adviser, can provide in managing demand for a revenue body.

Approaches to managing demand need to take into consideration the risks to revenue, compliance costs and administrative costs. Demand management does not mean providing a continuous supply of new services or additional resources.

Forward planning should be considered integral to effecting demand management strategies. This will allow a revenue body to understand its budget and resource constraints for delivering new services and to be more explicit about the 'trade-offs' and consequences when forming a position. It will also allow better marketing and communication to the community if there is a clear direction for the revenue body. In responding to demand, a revenue body may:

- invest in education programmes and products;
- review the number of channels through which services are offered and the options within the channels;
- better design policy or administrative procedures;
- review service standards;
- leverage from intermediaries.

Why manage demand?

Revenue bodies are required to work within a government framework of appropriate fiscal management and are faced with challenges in allocating their limited resources to meet organisational goals as well as meet citizen or business expectations of good service delivery and reduced compliance costs.

Effective demand management strategies can reduce organisational workload as well as improve taxpayer satisfaction by removing irritants.

All revenue bodies are faced with many different 'drivers' of demand that put pressure on an agency's resource allocation strategies and operating costs. Identifying the drivers and causes of demand and implementing cost-effective approaches to reduce or address them will benefit the revenue body through:

- more efficient allocation of resources to services of greatest need;
- delivering services more efficiently, including shifting services to less costly channels, such as self-service;
- reduction in compliance risks;
- savings in terms of budget;
- increased community support for the revenue system.

The benefits for the community are:

- better services and awareness for the community;
- reduced complexity;
- improved access;
- increasing confidence;
- greater consistency in services.

Related concepts for demand management

Channel management

A 'channel' is the access mechanism used by government to interact with customers and for customers to interact with government. Each channel and device has a unique set of attributes that make it suited to delivering particular services. Revenue bodies define their channel mix in several ways. Historically the most useful or common way to do this is by type. For example:

- **Online** – Electronic or digital channels, primarily a website, online forms, electronic data exchange systems and electronic messaging systems including e-mail and social media;
- **On-call** – The use of a phone system in providing services, such as contact centres and interactive voice recognition (IVR) systems;
- **On-paper** – Paper products being sent or received by the revenue body, including letters, brochures, forms, and faxes;
- **Face-to-face** – can be at a revenue body office or in the field, such as clients premises, third party premises, seminars, tradeshows, etc;
- **On-air** – External communications and marketing through media such as radio, television, press and other communication channels;
- **On-site** – Locations where members of the community can personally interact with revenue body staff in a one-to-many scenario, for example shop-fronts;
- **On-the-go** – Highly portable technologies that travel with people and can be used to interact with the revenue body, such as smart phones, mobiles, personal digital assistants (PDAs) and laptops.

The key to demand management is to understand the 'interactions' the revenue body has with their citizens, businesses and third parties/tax intermediaries. It requires a focus on identifying the 'root cause' or drivers of the interactions with the revenue body.

Broadly, the relationship between demand management and channel management can be viewed as follows:

- Demand Management is '**What** interactions the revenue body needs to support'; and
- Channel Management is '**How** the revenue body will support the interaction'.

It is important that a revenue body give consideration to establishing a channel strategy. A channel strategy is essential to manage demand effectively and should be reviewed every few years.

A channel strategy will outline the interaction or entry points the revenue body will need (and can afford) to have in place to support the community accessing the organisation's services. This will need to acknowledge that not all sections of the community can interact in the same way and a range of entry points may be needed. The strategy should also include a preferred channel, for example design services for the electronic channel in the first instance, and propose steps to shift or close channels that the revenue body will not support. The revenue body should also be cognisant that as technologies evolve and bring new opportunities, the cost of providing services will only decrease if channels are closed down. New channels can create fresh demand for services and often with high expectations for increasing speed of services. If existing channels continue to be maintained, the cost of providing service overall will simply increase.

Services

Services can be grouped into one of the following category types:

- Information Services – those services which include the provision of information such as general education, performance data, financial reports, press releases, policies, etc;
- Interaction Services – those services providing two way communication between an agency and a customer, that does not result in a change of account details or status (for example, general enquiries, account enquiries, debt and lodgement enquiries, technical advice, feedback);
- Transaction Services – those services which result in a change of a customer's account details or status (for example, lodgement of tax returns, registration, compliance activities, etc).
- Confirmation Services – those services that provide a confirmation that an activity on a customer's account has resulted in a change or provides a confirmation that the contact has been received.

The revenue body should also recognise that offering different service level standards across the different channels for the different service types can also be a way of managing demand.

Chapter 3

Managing service demand across a revenue body

The governance arrangements that a revenue body puts in place are important to the successful management of demand. This chapter describes the strategic framework and governance committees required to manage demand effectively.

Revenue bodies' strategic framework

Guiding principles and approaches

Revenue bodies have evolved a range of principles and approaches that guide their administration of tax laws, including the way they go about delivering services to taxpayers. These principles and approaches are generally reflected in the following types of revenue body documents:

- strategic plans/maps on organisational mission, vision, values, goals and objectives;
- high level business and risk management models;
- taxpayers' or service charters;
- service delivery standards.

As outlined in Box 3.1, such documents serve as a frame of reference for how revenue bodies should go about administering the tax system, including the management of service demand, to achieve improved outcomes (for example, increased community satisfaction with the quality of services delivered and improved cost effectiveness).

Box 3.1. Key strategic revenue body documents

Strategic statements of mission, vision, values, goals and objectives

Extracts of selected revenue bodies' strategic planning documents are set out in other documents produced by the Forum on Tax Administration. In terms of managing taxpayer service demand, the key points from such documents are as follows.

Statements of mission, in addition to a revenue body's role/mandate, frequently emphasise the broader societal role and benefits of a well-functioning tax system - that is, providing funds to support the services required for a civil society. As the community ultimately bears the costs of the services provided by a revenue body, citizens and businesses with tax-related responsibilities clearly expect they will receive high standards of service - value for money.

Revenue bodies' strategic plans or maps invariably contain an expression of the values (that is, norms of behaviour) that they aspire to demonstrate. These typically include integrity, professionalism/competence, mutual respect/trust, and fairness/procedural justice. Aspiring to achieve such values in practice must inevitably influence how revenue body officials are expected to interact with citizens and businesses in providing the services they need, and how they are equipped to carry out such responsibilities.

Box 3.1. Key strategic revenue body documents (*cont.*)

Revenue bodies' strategic goals and objectives tend to be relatively few in number and, in relation to tax administration, generally focus on improving taxpayers' compliance, increasing community satisfaction with the services delivered, attaining high levels of efficiency and strengthening internal capabilities. Such statements often set out quantified objectives and targets, including some that reflect organisational and community expectations of improvements in the standard of services delivered and the costs of providing them. Responsibility for achieving these strategic objectives and targets rests on those revenue body officials responsible for planning and executing service delivery.

Business and risk management models

Understanding the business and risk management models of the revenue body are important for service delivery. These models generally focus on understanding the environment the taxpayer operates in, providing a framework that makes it easy to comply and cost effective for the revenue body to administer and taking action and responding to behaviours that present risk to voluntary compliance. The service delivery framework – including response to demand pressures – needs to be cognisant always of the overarching outcomes of the revenue body and its approach to managing risk.

Taxpayers' or service charters

Charters define the relationship a revenue body seeks with the community – typically, a relationship based on mutual trust and respect. They outline taxpayers' rights and obligations under the law, as well as non-statutory commitments, direct the way the revenue body should behave towards the community, and tell the community what they can expect from the revenue body. Invariably, charters indicate that taxpayers are expected to be truthful and co-operative in their dealings with the revenue body, take reasonable care, and meet their tax obligations as they fall due.

The way taxpayers are treated, including by way of the quality of services provided to them, is an important factor in influencing their compliance behaviour. It is for this reason that charters often give emphasis to expectations of a revenue body in terms of:

1) treating taxpayers fairly and reasonably and as being honest in their tax affairs unless they have acted otherwise;
2) offering professional service and assistance to help taxpayers understand and meet their obligations;
3) engaging with taxpayers and their representatives; and
4) minimising the cost of compliance.

To be realised, such expectations must be taken account of in the design and delivery of service-focused programmes.

Service delivery standards

Statements of service delivery standards, sometimes embodied in revenue bodies' service charters, set out the service standards they seek to achieve. Typically these standards give emphasis to responsiveness for the major service-related processes undertaken by a revenue body (for example, all written inquiries answered in 20 work days, all VAT refunds processed in 20 work days). Achieving good levels of responsiveness for the major categories of service demanded by taxpayers doesn't 'just happen'. It requires careful planning and execution across all areas of a revenue body that are responsible for service delivery.

Source: Tax Administration in OECD and Selected Non-OECD Countries: Comparative Information Series (2010): www.oecd.org/tax/taxadministration/comparativeinformationseries2010.htm

Governance arrangements

Put simply, governance refers to the process of decision making and the process by which decisions are implemented. Good governance is the key to successful demand management.

This section outlines the governance arrangements required to manage demand effectively.

The revenue body's governance framework will be guided by:

- structure of the organisation – for example federated or highly centralised;
- nature of the revenue body's business – such as policy work or operations;
- range of business functions undertaken and the commonalities between them;
- requirements for communication and data sharing across the business functions of the revenue body and its partners;
- distribution of authority and the extent of central or local autonomy;
- procedures and responsibilities for business planning and defining business strategy;
- geographic distribution of organisational units, business functions and services providers such as IT;
- existence of corporate wide policies such as for purchasing and procurement;
- role and authority of cross organisational structures – for example executive steering groups in the revenue body and its partners;
- extent to which standards are enforced across the revenue body;
- extent to which work processes are common across the revenue body;
- internal controls and security policies.

Establishing clear governance arrangements is important so as to ensure organisational accountabilities are understood. An organisational approach to responding to demand pressures is considered necessary because the root cause or drivers of demand for services is often created by a different area of the revenue body than the one responding to the demand. As a consequence it is important to have a 'whole of revenue body' approach to reduce or eliminate the demand and to prioritise changes to services.

The case studies in Chapter 5 provide examples of the governance frameworks put in place by revenue bodies to manage demand.

Committees and roles that are important for effective demand management

This guide recommends the following organisational committees within the revenue body be put in place. This recommendation is based on feedback and experience of revenue bodies, recognising the importance of governance arrangements to service delivery and demand management and to ensure that relevant areas within the revenue body are engaged.

A key feature of a governance framework for service demand management is an overarching ***'Strategic Services Committee'*** that sets the strategic direction for service delivery in the revenue body. The strategy will reflect the revenue body's approach to demand for its services, including risk, cost, impact on compliance and the community. It also sets goals and objectives and measures for success. The committee provides advice to the revenue body's most senior executive group on priorities for service demand improvements, criteria for determining priorities and major strategies to eliminate/reduce demand. The committee should comprise senior executive of the revenue body.

This committee's role would be to:

- Define the service improvement outcomes the revenue body is seeking to achieve and sponsor these into the organisation's planning processes. For example these could include a mix of cost efficiency initiatives, improvements to compliance and responding to new policy requirements of government. The case study from Her Majesty's Revenue and Customs in the United Kingdom (refer Chapter 5) outlines three clear goals which they set for their demand management programme.
- Define the measures of success. For example 90% of services offered at the revenue body's on-site locations will be moved on line by 2013, 20% of phone calls on a particular topic will be eliminated and a further 20% moved to self-help on line.
- Define the revenue body's target groups.
- Define and prioritise the strategies that will be used to deliver these outcomes.

To do this the committee would:

- Be cognisant of the revenue body's vision and values when developing service strategy.
- Be representative of all areas within the revenue body and be committed to strategic end to end change.
- Monitor the success of the strategies and report on outcomes.
- Maintain a strategic focus of demand for services through a range of business intelligence inputs.
- Work very closely with the respective business and technology (where there is information technology support required) areas of the revenue body that supply the operational support. This is where the analysis will occur and change initiatives will come to life and be implemented.
- Ensure business areas report regularly to the Committee on the success (or otherwise) of the demand management initiatives.

Some examples of the roles that could be put in place and would be members of the Strategic Services Committee are:

- Channel Manager (Chair) – responsible for setting the strategic direction for how the channels of the revenue body will meet the demands of the community, expectations of government and ensure the revenue base is protected;
- Channel Owner – takes accountability to ensure that the revenue base is not adversely impacted by demand pressures in a particular channel and leads

organisational responses to minimise demand in that channel or assists to drive demand from other more costly channels;

- Product Owner – has organisational ownership for taxation (or social policy) products administered by the revenue body – for example Income Tax. This role has responsibility for the end to end administration of the product.

The Strategic Services Committee will be most effective if supported by an ***'Operational Services Committee'***. This committee would take an operational view, identifying demand management pressures and determining responses to demand drivers/causes and monitoring change initiatives. The committee understands the causes and linkages across the revenue body and recommends strategies to address the causes from a 'whole of revenue body' perspective. It also makes operational the strategies for service demand improvements, including setting measures, monitoring arrangements and reporting on the effectiveness of change initiatives. The committee's role would be to:

- understand the demand for services and the impact of the demand across the operational areas of the revenue body;
- oversee the implementation of service delivery strategies and respond to demand pressures for the revenue body;
- assess or analyse how well the service strategies are working and is able to respond quickly when the revenue body identifies contact or use of services that needs an immediate organisation response;
- put processes and procedures in place that allow the revenue body to understand how its services are being used, identify trends that are emerging and enable it to respond to demand pressures or change of direction quickly if needed;
- ensure priorities set by the Strategic Services Committee are managed through the organisation's change processes through to implementation;
- report regularly to the Strategic Services Committee on how successfully the overarching service strategies are being met;
- look for opportunities to invest savings from initiatives that reduce demand into other services, improvements or demand reduction strategies and make recommendations to the Strategic Services Committee.

The Operational Services Committee should have representation across relevant business areas, including areas that own the products and services that drive demand as well as the areas that manage the relationship with the clients and key stakeholders, for example individual taxpayers, small businesses and tax practitioners.

To understand how these committees can be used to manage demand, examples are provided from the Australian Taxation Office (see Annex A) and Ireland Revenue (see case study in Chapter 5).

Bibliography

OECD (2010), *Tax Administration in OECD and Selected Non-OECD Countries: Comparative Information Series*, OECD, Paris. *www.oecd.org/ctp/administration/CIS-2010.pdf*

Chapter 4

A framework for managing demand

This chapter outlines the phases and steps that a revenue body may take to assess the demand pressures on the revenue body's services and how this aligns with the revenue body's governance framework and compliance model.

The phases are Preparation, Analysis, Planning, and Implement and Evaluate.

Preparation phase

1. Know the revenue body's clients
2. Understand the costs
3. Understand the policy environment

Analysis phase

4. Identify Demand

Planning phase

5. Determine actions to be taken

Implement and evaluate phase

6. Implement a response
7. Monitor and evaluate

Demand management framework

How the steps fit in with the governance approach is depicted in the following diagram. The demand management framework is a continuous cycle, as it is important for a revenue body to continually evaluate and re-assess the social, economic and technological environment within which it operates. For example changes in client behaviour, budget cuts and changes to the law could impact on demand for the revenue body's services. The steps may be applied partially or passed over, depending on the scale of the demand management change initiative and/or direction from the Strategic Services Committee.

Figure 4.1. Demand management framework

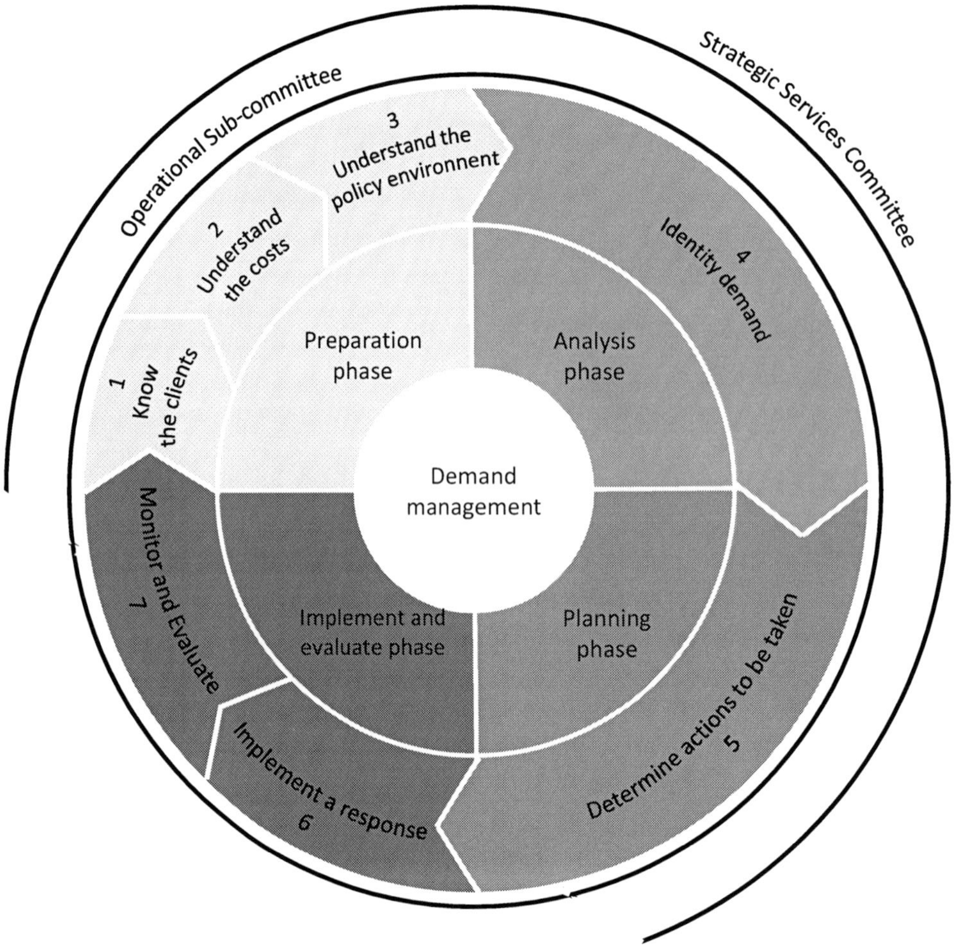

Source: FTA's Taxpayer Services sub-group

Preparation phase

Step 1 – Know the revenue body's clients

Demand management strategies require a good knowledge of the revenue body's clients' needs, motivations, expectations, including challenges in dealing with the revenue body, and operating procedures. Client attitudes to the revenue body, the service offered, their values and other factors, such as the social, economic and technological environment they live in, will affect whether they will participate in and support demand management initiatives. The decisions of clients to accept (or oppose) changes to services as a result of demand management initiatives will be influenced by how they perceive the changes will affect them.

At a minimum, the revenue body will need to look at its taxpayer base according to the laws it administers, client characteristics and behaviours. Clients can, for example, be categorised as individuals, small business and large business or tax professionals and intermediaries. Each category can be further segmented by demographic, for example individuals could be young adults, employees, pensioners etc. Clients can also be segmented on behaviour – what are the client group's needs? And what is the risk to revenue?

Categorising the client base enables a revenue body to better service its clients and provides the basic information required to evaluate and distinguish 'needs' from 'wants' and ultimately the demand for services.

Through the revenue body's intelligence and risk processes, it is important to identify the clients that will not comply, regardless of the services put in place. This is where demand management, service delivery and compliance strategies need to be considered 'holistically' from a whole of revenue body perspective. This will be where the Strategic Services Committee will play a prominent role.

Strategies to facilitate change can also be influenced by good communication and education and the marketing of alternative service delivery channels. If a revenue body can 'promote' the change and explain the value to the client it can improve the revenue body's clients' participation (and partnership) in the revenue system.

There is also increasing interest from the community to more simply access government services across the various agencies (and levels) of government. The revenue body's service delivery strategies should enable this approach and look to either lead a whole of government approach for a particular service or work with other government agencies to leverage opportunities.

To understand the revenue body's clients, the revenue body may consider a range of approaches that are described briefly in Table 4.1.

Table 4.1. Approaches for understanding the revenue body's clients

Approaches that can be taken	Description
Seeking clients' direct feedback on offered services	Revenue bodies should consider making it as easy as possible for clients to provide feedback about their experience interacting with the revenue body's brand, products or services. A client should be able to share their experience at every touch point such as websites, through feedback cards, e-mail, call centres and other direct forms of contact.
Using online communities	Participation in online communities provides another way in which revenue bodies can seek feedback and understand what drives their clients.
Mining external social media sites for clients opinions and sentiments	Sites, forums and blogs are another rich source of feedback. Revenue bodies can glean insights that may not be available in the organisation's formal feedback methods.
Capturing feedback in a structured way	The collection of structured data through an online form or survey should be considered. However, it should not encumber the client with privacy concerns or be over burdensome. A good rule of thumb is no more than 10 explicit attributes (for example, name, e-mail address, contact type, channel, experience, etc).
Responding to clients feedback	As important as it is to collect information from the revenue body's clients it is just as important to respond and acknowledge their input.

Table 4.1. Approaches for understanding the revenue body's clients (*cont.*)

Approaches that can be taken	Description
Using intelligence from the revenue bodies intelligence and risk processes	A revenue body captures intelligence on the compliance behaviour of its clients through its administration. This information is a good indicator to how well a revenue body's service and compliance strategies are aligning and making it easy for the community to comply.
Conducting user research	Involving taxpayers in the planning, design, development and implementation of services ensures any changes deliver on their business intent, provide benefits to the government and the revenue body and is useful and usable for the taxpayer. User research techniques could include: • focus groups – a discussion with a group of taxpayers about a product or idea; • collaborative design session – developing a prototype of a product with a small group of taxpayers; • prototyping – a walkthrough of a system with taxpayers using a HTML, PowerPoint version or paper copy of the products or screens; • user interviews – a one-on-one interview with a taxpayer to evaluate a product, process or system; • use ability testing – an evaluation of a product or system by the taxpayer who are observed whilst interacting with the product, and • personas – a persona is a fictional user created to represent a client group.

Understand client interactions

Understanding all the revenue body's interactions, the drivers of these interactions and the value they provide to the taxpayer and the revenue body is essential to the development of an effective demand management approach. Establishing this requires development of an overall catalogue of interaction types across the revenue body in a way that allows statistics to be collected and analysis to occur. Statistics can be gathered through such methods such as call management systems, hits on a website, downloads from web pages, website log-ins, number of face-to-face appointments. This analysis must identify the reasons for the interaction and drive out aspects such as if the interaction is 'prescribed' in a particular way such as by a form or piece of correspondence.

The additional piece of work (and key to good demand management) is the ability to classify the value of the interaction from a compliance or organisational perspective. Finland's National Board of Taxes uses the model depicted in Box 4.1 to classify their client interactions.

Box 4.1. Example of a model to understand client interactions

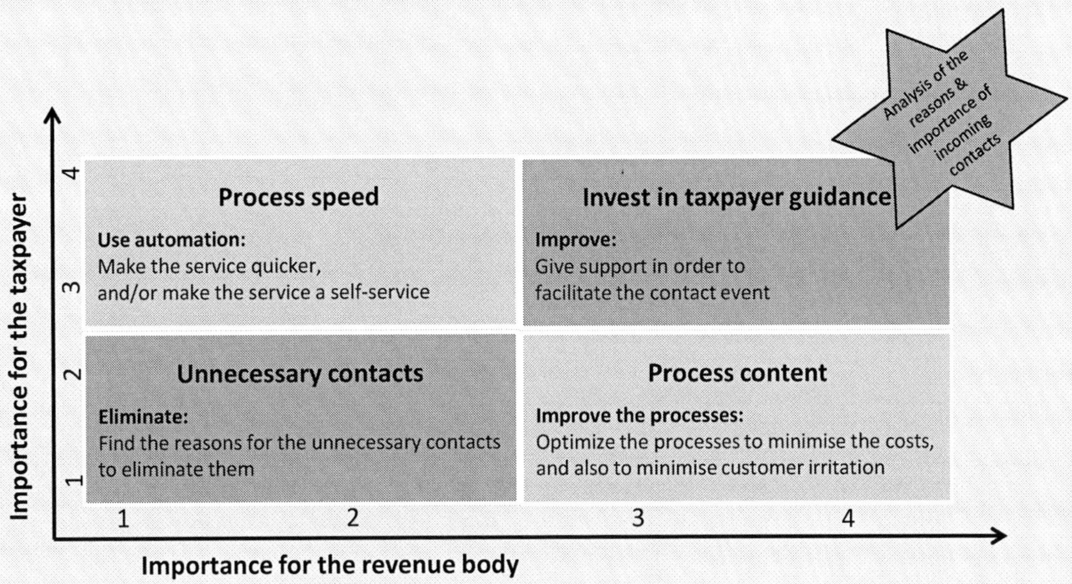

Source: National Board of Taxes, Finland

Step 2 – Understand the costs

Know the revenue body's channels

It is essential that a revenue body understands the channels through which services are provided to taxpayers, including the cost, maintenance and effectiveness of each channel to encourage voluntary compliance and make it simpler for a taxpayer to access services and interact with the revenue body.

Each channel has a channel owner. The channel owners are the business representatives with responsibility for overseeing the delivery of service strategies within their channels and the need to understand the costs to support their channels.

The revenue body's Strategic Services Committee should also have a sound understanding of the revenue body's channel strategy, the services offered within the channel and the costs of supporting these services.

This Committee should also have a good understanding of how each client group interacts with the revenue body's channel strategy. For example young adults are highly active (and competent) in the mobile device space and prefer to deal with services provided through this platform. The senior population may still have a high dependency on paper. Client behaviours may also change over time, for example Denmark have seen an increase in electronic interactions in the over 60s age group.

In understanding the cost of each channel the Strategic Services Committee should have information outlining the full costs, for example the design and build of a web service or the delivery of a paper product and the print costs, as well as access to information about responses and time required to bring a new product or channel to market. This should also address the type of service each channel can support, with consideration given to whether the channel is designed for single to multiple type interactions or if it can manage bulk interactions.

Table 4.2 provides an extract from a recent Audit Report on New Zealand Inland Revenue department highlighting the significant cost differential that can be experienced across channels – noting that online costs were not available at the time.

Table 4.2. Example of channel costs

Channel	Number of Interactions	Total Direct Cost $	Cost per transaction $
Telephone	3 077 767	94 698 724	30.77
Correspondence	1 062 780	44 108 116	41.50
Counter	180 116	8 604 424	47.77

Source: Figure 5 – Cost of communication channels from July 2010 to April 2011, p. 19, Performance audit report Inland Revenue Department: Making it easy to comply, New Zealand Controller and Auditor-General-*www.oag.govt.nz/2011/making-it-easy-to-comply/docs/ird-making-it-easy-to-comply.pdf/view*

Step 3 - Understand the policy environment

The policy environment may challenge the revenue body's ability to implement strategies to manage demand. Policy and legislative complexities could be that the law requires a tax administration office (face to face centre) to be located within a certain distance from where the taxpayer resides, a requirement to send paper assessment notices or that the revenue body administers both the tax and social/welfare systems. Within these constraints, a revenue body should consider the role that design plays in developing and implementing solutions that achieve a balance between government policy, the revenue body's administration of the law and the taxpayers ability to comply.

The case studies in Chapter 5 provide examples of the preparation phase steps revenue bodies take to manage demand.

Analysis phase

Step 4 – Identify demand

Anticipate where practical

Revenue bodies should consider where practical, implementing processes that predict potential problems before they occur or become difficult to resolve. Problems can be identified through regular monitoring and reporting of volume 'peaks' of the revenue body's services.

There is potential to link a revenue body's 'incident' and 'problem' management to the demand management governance with the outcome that new emerging volumes could be considered and managed more effectively. If this was put in place the Operational Services Committee would be able to use the intelligence to make decisions and recommendations on where the 'root cause analysis' work should be focused.

To assist revenue bodies anticipate demand, a tool such as the Information Technology Infrastructure Library (ITIL) provides a worldwide recognised framework that allows an organisation to monitor and manage services.

Understand the drivers of demand

Drivers of demand for service can be many and varied. For example, service demand is often highest in the tax lodgement season. Letter campaigns or communication strategies from the revenue body, media, government policy, election promises or events such as natural disasters or economic downturn can also create service demand.

A revenue body needs to conduct analysis to identify the drivers, in order to:

- understand the revenue body's priority services;
- distinguish 'needs' from 'wants or expectations';
- determine the true costs of providing those services;
- determine the value add the service is providing. 'low' or 'no value' contacts should be targeted for removal. For example, is the demand for information only or does it require action from the revenue body;
- identify interactions that are caused by errors in revenue body administration, for example poorly designed procedures and processes. This can also lead to multiple contacts as clients 'shop' until they get the answer they want;
- monitor for newly emerging demand (increasing numbers of interactions would be an indicator).

Operational areas of the revenue body will need to report regularly on the use, cost and demand for the revenue body's services. This reporting should ideally report 'hot spots' or trends that are occurring that may benefit from further analysis.

Box 4.2. Example of understanding the drivers of demand

Each year, the Netherlands Tax and Customs Administration carries out a Customer Satisfaction Survey among its customers to find out their opinion about the services provided to them.

One of the questions in the survey was the number of calls the customer made to get the service or the product they needed. The survey showed that 20% of the customers were responsible for 60% of the call volume. As a result the Taxpayer Services of the Netherlands Tax and Customs Administration commenced a Lean Six Sigma project.

The business consultants made a list of customers who called 3, 4, 5 ... up to 10 times within a 6-week period. A team of four call centre representatives contacted the customers ('outbound calling') and asked them why they had called on three or more occasions. A total of 500 customers were contacted over a four week period. The business consultants analysed the data of the 'outbound calling' and found the main reasons for repeated calls were connected to the procedure for requesting the "IB-60" form which states the income of the applicant. An IB-60 is used for instances such as renting a house. Each year 400 000 customers apply for an IB-60 form.

The business consultants mapped the internal business process together with the back-office and found that there were two main reasons for requesting the IB-60 form multiple times. The first reason was that the process took seven working days instead of the published five days. The second was that the Interactive Voice Response System (IVR) was not adequate in its feedback, for example the message was 'We have got your order and you will get a reply within five working days.'

Two process changes were made. Firstly, the postal delivery process was changed so that the application would be delivered within five working days by changing the 48 hours delivery service into a 24 hours turnaround. Secondly, the IVR message was changed to 'We have got a request order for an IB-60 for the year [Application Year] and within 5 working days you will get the statement.'

Five months after implementing the changes, the number of repeat calls had decreased from 3.6% to 0.6% due to the quicker postal delivery resulting in a benefit of approximately EUR 58 800 (total cost of the 24 hour mail services is EUR 14 000). As a result of the IVR changes, the number of repeat calls had dropped by 40% resulting in a benefit of approximately EUR 21 000 (the total cost of the new IVR recording being EUR 300).

Source: Netherlands Tax and Customs Administration

Prioritise what the revenue body will analyse

A revenue body will generally have many services that require monitoring and analysing to determine if they are achieving their desired outcomes. The resources and tools available to conduct this monitoring/analysis will also generally be limited in capacity or availability so it is important that a 'whole of revenue body' approach be taken to prioritising what will be analysed in more depth.

The Operational Service Committee and Strategic Services Committee will play an important role to achieve this. These groups will be aware of the revenue body goals and strategy and needs to determine which areas (topics) of the revenue body's business need to be focused on as a priority.

For major legislative changes, the Strategic Services Committee would prioritise monitoring and analysis of demand for services through the call centre, correspondence and the website to ensure that education material is being understood and whether the education products need adjusting to reduce the need for client interactions.

Box 4.3. Example of prioritising demand for services for analysis

The Australian Taxation Office (ATO) is undertaking a significant Superannuation Reform Programme in response to the government announcement of a range of changes to Australia's superannuation (retirement income) system. One aspect of the Programme involves writing to the Superannuation industry to explain what the changes will mean to the industry and what they need to do to comply with the new obligations and refers them to further information on the ATO's website. As the Programme will mean significant changes over a seven year period, the Service Improvement Steering Committee has prioritised the Program me as an analysis piece to determine if the strategies to inform and prepare the industry, are working. The analysis will look at what has worked as well as any unintended consequences, such as increased phone calls due to inadequate or incomplete information on the website.

Source: Australian Taxation Office

For more operational issues such as 'incidents' or 'problems' identified through regular monitoring of the revenue bodies services, the Operational Service Committee will play more of a part. For example an increase in a particular call type greater than was expected outside peak processing may need to be assessed for the root cause.

Identify the root cause of the interaction

It is important for a revenue body to develop capability to analyse the demand for services. Business analysts often from the operational areas of the revenue body would undertake this work. Analysis is very important to understand why the taxpayer is interacting with the revenue body and to determine the 'root cause' of the interaction.

There are some taxpayer interactions a revenue body will want. For example the use of calculators on the revenue body's website that allows employers to calculate withholding rates for their employees or estimate the payments required under a payment arrangement. Use of these services is encouraged as they are interactions that use the revenue body's 'self-help' services.

Interactions that a revenue body may not want are low value or expensive to service. A good example of this would be where the revenue body offers an online product on its website that is not working effectively. However, use of tools and feedback from call centre staff highlights that there has been a significant increase in information requests over the phone channel about the online product because it is not well designed and clients do not understand what they need to do. The product also directs clients to the phone if they want more information. It is clear in this case that analysis has identified why the interaction is occurring and that a poorly designed online product is causing a low value or unwanted contact to occur. The online product was intended to enable self-help, but failed.

It is also possible that a root cause for a contact can be driven by the complexity in the law. In this case there may be little a revenue body can do except to put processes in place to influence the design of policy and legislation with the relevant government authority or minister. The design should highlight the taxpayer's ability to comply and the revenue bodies' ability to administer the policy or legislation.

An example of review cycles and analysis undertaken by Inland Revenue Authority of Singapore is provided in Chapter 5.

Tools and techniques

Some examples of the tools and techniques an analyst can use to identify how well the revenue body's strategies are working and identify if any problems that need addressing are:

- ***Speech Analytics*** – Automated tools that can mine, categorise and analyse unstructured audio into dialogue. These types of tools are sophisticated in nature and will require information technology investment. An example of a case study using the Verint Speech Analytics tool in the Australian Taxation Office is provided in Chapter 5.
- ***Voice of the Customer (VOC) Postcards*** – this is a manual process and less sophisticated in nature. This process is employed in the United Kingdom and involves a group of advisors classifying each of their calls into categories that reflect the reason for the call in the 'voice' of the customer. This provides qualitative analysis and allows the revenue body to report on the 'root causes' for the call.
- ***Use of Surveys*** – Ireland Revenue has recently used a survey approach to understand the reasons customers have contacted them for particular tax types or products. Again this is an easy way of targeting how well the revenue body's service delivery strategies are working.
- ***Online Communities*** – participation in online communities can not only help the revenue body to better get to know their clients, it can also identify how well the services are meeting their needs. It can be a good source of knowledge to gain intelligence such as '*…I was forced to ring the revenue body the other day because…*'

Table 4.3. Example of tool used to determine root causes of a demand pressure created by the revenue body

Examples	Description
Importance of understanding the root cause	A revenue body receives a significant increase in phone calls during the peak processing period. They are for a contact type that was not expected or planned for. Using a voice analytics tool it was found that the reason the taxpayer was contacting the revenue body was that a debt letter campaign was initiated requesting the taxpayer to contact the revenue body to set up a payment arrangement if they were to avoid further penalties and interest being applied to their debt.
Learning for the revenue body	Rather than immediately react and look at processes to bring more staff on board (or shift from other work activities) a better response would be to stop the letters. An out-bound call campaign or a self-help online facility may have generated a better outcome. A revenue body needs to be careful that it doesn't just shift the resource burden to another part of the organisation without considering the broader implications.

Box 4.4. Example of determining the root cause

A taxpayer may initiate a call to a revenue body's call centre to obtain a business identifier. From a topic/driver perspective, this call would be classified as a request for a business number or business registration.

However, to determine the 'root cause' the revenue body needs to understand precisely why the taxpayer decided to call and speak with an agent when they could have used the online business registration system or sent in a request by mail instead.

More specifically, the revenue body needs to determine why these other methods may not have been considered by the taxpayer. For example, was it because:

- There was a lack of awareness of the other methods available? In this case the mitigation strategy may need to include better marketing.
- The online system was difficult to use? This may lead us to suggesting changes to the online system.
- The documentation in the paper registration kit was difficult to understand or left questions unanswered? That would require a rewrite of the information.
- The taxpayer required a business identifier on an urgent basis and decided that the quickest way of obtaining it would be to call and speak to an agent? That could suggest a realignment of service standards to make the online issuance of a business identifier the fastest service.
- The taxpayer was advised by some external organisation to call the number? This could mean ensuring that the external organisation has the right information.

Once the underlying reason or cause for the contact has been determined, the revenue body will be in a much better position to affect positive change. Understanding demand needs to go beyond establishing topics or drivers of contacts. It is only by determining the true root cause of contacts that the revenue body will be able to influence those contacts in the future.

Source: OECD (2012), *Working smarter in revenue administration – Using demand management strategies to meet service delivery goals*, OECD, Paris. *www.oecd.org/site/ctpfta/49428187.pdf*

What is the value of the interaction?

Identifying low value interactions is an important element of identifying and prioritising demand management opportunities. This can include:

- stakeholder discussions, particularly with process or product owners within the revenue body;
- stakeholder discussions with intermediaries, taxpayer focus groups or other taxpayer research;
- current reporting of outcomes relating to particular interactions;
- assessing the impact of the contact on compliance and revenue;
- assessing the cost of delivering the interaction, such as channel and staffing costs, and the benefit of continuing to deliver the interaction in the same way or shifting or removing the interaction.

What does the analysis phase deliver?

At the end of the analysis phase the revenue body should have enough information to understand if the strategies are on track or whether a different response is required.

The case studies in Chapter 5 provide examples of the analysis phase steps revenue bodies take to manage demand.

Planning phase

Step 5 – Determine actions to be taken

Undertake design

To determine the right approach (or solution) to respond to a demand pressure it is important to undertake design following the analysis phase. Ideally this would be managed with the business area that has identified the problem and the design area of the revenue body.

The design process to develop the solution is very important as good design will help identify and eliminate unintended consequences of changes the revenue body makes. Design should look at the client experience trying to be achieved and how the revenue body will need to respond – from an administrative, policy and technology perspective – to meet the outcome.

An effective design process will involve key subject matter experts and business areas to ensure a whole of organisation assessment of the change is made. This includes what it means for the client group to interact with the change, the revenue body's ability to support (and afford) the change and the risks or obstacles in implementing the change.

This process will identify potential products, processes, system and policy (maybe even legal) changes that are needed to support the outcome. For example an income tax form may need changing (or a new one developed). This will generally involve appropriate endorsement from the product owner (if they exist). It is important to do the design and identify these types of impacts.

When determining a response the revenue body should be prepared to experiment to see what works (and what doesn't) and take an iterative approach to refine processes and services. Small steps can be taken – the revenue body doesn't need to achieve a perfect solution straight away and can chip away at the demand drivers.

If a more formal approach is required then the Operational Services Committee has the role to sponsor the change project into the business areas to lead and work with the design area of the revenue body.

Determine options to respond to a demand pressure

There is not always one single solution to manage a response to a demand pressure. The design phase will help identify the optimal solution. In many cases a range of strategies will often be more successful than a single strategy.

Table 4.4. Options for shifting service demand

Strategy	Purpose
Reduce the underlying need for the contact	The revenue body may (inadvertently) create the demand by corresponding with taxpayers and asking them to contact the revenue body rather than contacting the taxpayer directly in the first place. Redesign of letters may reduce confusion and questions that are currently causing taxpayers to contact the revenue body. The revenue body's website may have content on a topic that is not clear, causing the taxpayer to call for clarification.
Invest in education	Establish a marketing and communication programme that lets taxpayers know about the services you provide and how they can access them. The marketing and communication programme should focus on the revenue body's preferred channel (such as self-help) and the benefit for the taxpayer in using that channel. Depending on the revenue body's (and taxpayers) capability this can be done in a variety of ways through use of social media or video/on air services. Incentives could be offered to shift to preferred channels, such as reduced process time for income tax returns if filed on line.
Review change management procedures	Examine the administrative and management practices in place to deliver the services. Try and identify the 'levers' you control. This would look at challenging decisions that potentially create an unwanted or unplanned demand on your resources.
Review services	Re-design related services where two contacts/transactions are currently required so that one combined interaction can satisfy the need. Alternatively it could be about risk assessing the value of certain procedures to determine if the cost of a current process requiring contact can be justified against the compliance or revenue outcomes. It should be noted that tailoring information and services to client segment may also help eliminate and manage demand.
Review channel choice	The service could be one you support but is being offered in a more expensive channel and the revenue body may need to identify alternate channels to offer the service. Alternatively, decisions could be made to close a channel, such as face-to-face, and shifting clients to more efficient and cost effective channels, such as on line and on-call. This could be done by establishing a channel strategy that includes principles about designing services for the electronic (self-help) channel in the first instance or mandating the electronic/online channel.
Invest in assets	Identify and build/purchase tools that can help the agency identify demand and provide greater provision of self-service options to the community.
Review service standards	Aim to influence demand by reviewing your services and the standards that apply to them. For more costly channels (for example paper) it may be suitable to have longer service standards than in the preferred electronic channels such as online portals – providing the incentive to go on line.
Leverage the accounting and tax professional or intermediaries	Accountants and Tax Professionals can help manage the demand. They have established relationships with the community and understand their clients. Working closely with them and leveraging their natural networks to implement change can be very cost effective and simple to put in practice.
Better designed policy	Use an integrated design approach to tax policy design, development and implementation that meets the needs of government and makes it easy for taxpayer/citizen to comply.

Examples of different options put in place by revenue bodies are provided in Japan's National Tax Agency and New Zealand Inland Revenue's case studies in Chapter 5.

Box 4.5. Example of leveraging from intermediaries to manage demand

In Denmark the police traditionally registered motor vehicles and delivered number-plates to car dealerships or the individual owner of the vehicle. A few years ago, on a decision made by Parliament, the Ministry of Taxation was tasked with the objective of reducing the cost of managing registrations.

The change involved developing an advanced IT-system and outsourcing the registration and number-plate handling to authorised private companies ('platehandler') such as car dealerships, vehicle inspectors etc.

Authorised 'platehandlers' are obliged to operate for set days/times and are the first point of contact for the customer. In this way the Danish tax authority has reduced the service demand from the consumer by outsourcing to a third party.

Source: Central Customs and Tax Administration, Denmark

Revenue bodies need to manage the risk to revenue however this must be balanced with the need to provide the right services in the right channels and to encourage participation in the revenue system.

Evaluating options

The Operational Services Committee will play an important role in evaluating options. It will contain the business and informational technology representatives that will understand the service strategies and will have the 'links' into the business that monitors and analyses the services. This sub-committee will understand what works well (and what doesn't).

Recommending an approach

- The Operational Services Committee needs to prioritise change ideas and make recommendations to the Strategic Services Committee for endorsement. Knowing the strategic direction and change agenda for the revenue body, the Strategic Services Committee needs to consider whether the change idea is of sufficient importance to feed into the broader revenue body change agenda.
- The Strategic Services Committee and Operational Services Committee will also need to be aware of issues such as the capacity and budgetary restraints of the revenue body. There will be resource issues to consider (particularly relevant for any change with information technology requirements) and the revenue body's ability to administer them. They will need to manage expectations, both within the revenue body and that of the taxpayers. For example, in the Australian Taxation Office there is a separate executive committee that looks after the budget for information technology investment. The Strategic Services Committee works closely with this committee to understand what changes can be undertaken.
- It is highly unlikely that the revenue body will be able to implement every change initiative or respond to every demand pressure so it is important a prioritisation phase is undertaken. The Strategic Services Committee may need to sponsor service improvement initiatives into planning and change processes.

- To help the committee measure and compare the relative priorities a business case should be developed by the sponsoring business area under the guidance of the Operational Services Committee. The business case considers aspects such as:

  - links to the revenue body's strategic outcomes;

  - is there a significant revenue or reputational risk identified?

  - is there a client experience the revenue body is trying to achieve?

  - could the implementation of the change be done through a phased approach, across a number of years?

  - what is the change initiative targeting?

    – reducing service demand - eliminating unnecessary contact;

    – shifting service demand - offering improved self-service options on line and removing the burden from the phone or paper channels;

    – managing peak demand - largely driven by legislated obligations. This would generally be a priority area for a revenue body, and

    – whole of government - whether the change to the interaction is broader than the revenue body. For example, interactions with the social policy/welfare system or a broader whole of government approach to simplify service delivery for citizens such as a service to notify change of citizen contact details for all government agencies.

The case studies in Chapter 5 provide examples of the planning phase steps revenue bodies take to manage demand.

Implementation and evaluation phase

Step 6 – Implement a response

It is at this step that the revenue body actually implements the design recommended by the Operational Services Committee and endorsed by the Strategic Services Committee.

Usually a business sponsor (and project manager) would be appointed if the change is of enough significance to warrant a formal project to be established. The business sponsor is responsible for preparing the project plan for all the business deliverables (including design documents) and working with the information technology project manager to understand all the information technology dependencies.

Essentially, there will be a need to follow the project management methodology that exists for the revenue body. If the revenue body doesn't have a methodology there a number of modern methodologies available, for example Prince 2[1] or PRISM[2].

Step 7 – Monitor, evaluate and report

This step provides information on the need to evaluate the change made and to continually monitor the success of the revenue body's demand management strategies.

Monitor

To monitor the ongoing process, a revenue body needs to:

- understand the outcomes being sought by the demand management response;
- develop the metrics. Where quantitative measures are desired, data will need to be collected and assessed to identify changes in demand directly attributable to the selected demand management initiatives;
- have the right analyst skills in place to monitor the demand, understand patterns and trends and issues arising, and
- establish appropriate reporting processes to the Operational Services Committee and Strategic Services Committee.

It is important to continually review the impacts of any change on the revenue body's clients. If there were unforeseen consequences of the initiative that caused the revenue body's client group to disengage from the revenue system or experience hardship then these need to be identified early and addressed.

Evaluate

This is an important step in the demand management process, as it helps the revenue body determine the success of the change. It also puts in place ongoing processes to monitor demand and highlight any issues that might arise in the future.

To evaluate the success of the change, a revenue body needs to conduct a review to determine:

- Whether the desired outcome achieved. Has the outcome resulted in benefits or savings? Has there been any adverse (or desired) impact on revenue?
- Whether the revenue body achieved the desired shift in demand;
- Whether there have been any unexpected outcomes such as moving the demand from one type of service or product to another;
- Lessons learned.

Report

The outcome of the monitor and evaluate step should be reported by the respective business areas to the Operational Services Committee and, where necessary, the Strategic Services Committee. Depending on the size of the change initiative, reporting may be on a quarterly or half yearly basis.

The report should outline progress against:

- the measures attached to each of the strategies and whether on track;
- the effectiveness of the strategies and benefits to taxpayers and the revenue body such as improving taxpayer satisfaction with the service, timeliness, accessibility, quality and reduced costs;
- any new or emerging risks as a result of the change initiatives implemented.

The case studies in Chapter 5 provide examples of the implement and evaluate phase steps revenue bodies take to manage demand.

Notes

1. PRINCE2 (an acronym for PRojects IN Controlled Environments) is a de facto process-based method for effective project management. Used extensively by the UK Government, PRINCE2 is also widely recognised and used in the private sector, both in the UK and internationally. The PRINCE2 method is in the public domain, and offers non-proprietorial best practice guidance on project management.

2. PRISM is a process-based, structured project management methodology that introduces areas of sustainability and integrates them into four core project phases in order to maximize opportunities to improve sustainability and the use of finite resources. The methodology encompasses the management, control and organization of a project with consideration and emphasis beyond the project life-cycle and on the five aspects of sustainability, People, Planet, Profit, Process and Product. It derives the framework from ISO: 21500 as well as ISO 14001, ISO 26000, and ISO 9001 PRISM is also used to refer to the training and accreditation of authorized practitioners of the methodology who must undertake accredited qualifications based on competency to obtain the GPM certification.

Bibliography

OECD (2012), *Working smarter in revenue administration – Using demand management strategies to meet service delivery goals*, OECD, Paris. *www.oecd.org/site/ctpfta/49428187.pdf*

Inland Revenue Department (2011), *Cost of communication channels from July 2010 to April 2011,* Performance audit report Inland Revenue Department: Making it easy to comply, New Zealand Controller and Auditor-General, p. 19. *www.oag.govt.nz/2011/making-it-easy-to-comply/docs/ird-making-it-easy-to-comply.pdf/view*

Chapter 5

Case studies

Australian Taxation Office - Governance and use of a speech analytics tool (Verint)

Background

The Australian Tax Office (ATO) receives over 11 million calls each year. Although all calls are recorded for quality assurance purposes, it is not possible to listen to them all.

In late 2011, the ATO implemented new technology to better understand taxpayers needs, improve its service and detect potential scams. The technology (a speech analytics tool - Verint) scans for key words (categories) and phrases in millions of call recordings and assists the ATO to respond to emerging trends.

There are six stages in the process to establish a category in the speech analytics tool.

- establish predetermined categories (for example topics/areas of interest);
- determine unique words that relate to the category;
- speech analytics capture all contacts that have the requested 'unique' words within the call;
- an analyst listens to a sample of the calls to ensure relevance of the category;
- if there is a 93% success rate (that is, that the call is relevant to the category) that can be established from the sampling, then the category is published, and
- once established the category can be utilised for ongoing analysis.

Governance mechanisms

A small team in the Customer Service & Solutions (CS&S) business line are responsible for the administration of Verint in the ATO. The head of CS&S is a member of the Service Improvement Steering Committee, the strategic body in the ATO that reports and makes recommendations to the ATO Executive Committee on ATO service strategy progress, outcomes, risks and issues, providing assurance that ATO service improvements have appropriate strategic level corporate governance. CS&S business line provide frontline services, across a range of channels including telephone, correspondence and social media, to tax practitioners and the community (taxpayers). A CS&S representative is also a member of the Service Improvement Sub-Committee which provides input and support to the Service Improvement Steering Committee and is responsible for identifying and progressing opportunities to improve service delivery, supporting the ATO's channel strategy including maximising opportunities to shift to preferred service channels and identifying and responding to demand pressures.

As a test case for the new speech analytics tool, the team in CS&S selected 'Superannuation Guarantee' (SG) as a category and carried out an analysis of calls for the period December to March 2012. Superannuation is money set aside over a person's lifetime to provide for their retirement. For most people, superannuation begins when they start work and their employer starts paying superannuation for them – these payments are known as superannuation guarantee contributions.

The analysis was provided to the Superannuation business line's Executive in April 2012. Superannuation business line (as a 'product' owner) is responsible for the design and administration of Australia's Superannuation (retirement income) system and making it easier for the taxpayers to comply with the laws that govern superannuation.

The Superannuation Executive asked that further analysis be done during the TaxTime (income tax filing) period to see if there were any re-occurring themes. This analysis was conducted for the period 1 July 2012 and 30 September 2012 and presented to the Superannuation Executive.

Analysis

An analysis of the July - September 2012 compared to the December - March 2012 period found that there were many more calls during this period and the call lengths were longer.

- In July - September there were 9 809 calls (an average of 3 270 per month) and average talk time was 5:21 minutes.
- In December - March there were 3 528 calls (an average of about 931 per month) and average talk time was 4:41 minutes.
- Half of the calls were from employees:
  - In July - September 53% of calls were from employees;
  - In December - March 60% of calls were from employees.
- In December - March, about half (53%) of the calls were employees questioning whether their employers were contributing enough superannuation, and only 16% were about how salary sacrifice relates to Superannuation Guarantee.
- In July - September, about half (54%) of the calls were about salary sacrifice and its relationship to superannuation or salary packaging (and no calls were about whether employers were contributing enough superannuation).
- Partly because of the complexity of salary sacrifice arrangements, it was assessed that two-thirds of calls were longer than required and that incomplete information was provided in about half (47%) of the calls.

What was the outcome?

As a result of the analysis, a number of recommendations were developed and discussed with the Superannuation and CS&S Executive:

- Regular scenario based training sessions provided to Superannuation trained staff in small groups during either team meetings or in group based learning and development sessions. These sessions could use role plays to improve questioning and clarifying, ensure paraphrasing for understanding, and teach script interpretation to improve talk time, customer satisfaction and quality.

- Team leaders, senior advisors, and/or service consultants with appropriate skills listen to the calls across the site for questioning, clarifying and paraphrasing for understanding.
- Customer service representative's with excellent skills in these areas are to be used as 'champions' to improve these skills for other customer service representatives across ATO call centres.

These recommendations are now being progressed through CS&S.

Lessons learnt

A whole of agency approach to demand management as well as effective governance structures need to be in place. Often the root cause or drivers of demand are created by a different area within the revenue body than the one responding to the demand. Strategies to address demand may require changes to information published on the website, a change to the channel/s for delivering the services or the design and implementation of an information technology solution.

Japan National Tax Agency (NTA) - Response to the Great East Japan earthquake

Background

The Great East Japan earthquake on 11 March 2011 caused enormous damage. It also significantly affected the Japanese tax administration resulting in damage to some office buildings and interrupting day-to-day operations.

Since then, the Japanese tax administration continues to work on the issues related to the earthquake, such as establishing a special administration system for taxpayers who suffered from the disaster.

What was the problem?

The number of such natural disasters has increased all over the world in recent years. The response of tax administrations to these disasters will significantly affect the trust in tax administrations from the public and taxpayers, as well as those who were directly affected by the natural disaster. Accordingly, the NTA places extra high priorities on dealing with demand management in emergencies such as earthquake related issues.

How did the NTA develop a response/solution to the problem?

As an immediate response following the earthquake, the NTA promptly extended the deadlines for tax filings, payments, etc. The deadline for individual tax returns was 15 March and the earthquake happened right before the deadline.

In the affected areas, the NTA publicised and notified taxpayers of the special tax treatments for losses caused by the earthquake. Subsequently, taxpayers who suffered from the disaster were evacuated all over Japan, so the NTA implemented a publicity and notifications campaign in local tax offices throughout the country, by providing relevant material and conducting training sessions for tax officials.

On 27 April 2011, a special tax implementation law for the disaster was enacted and implemented, which allows a deduction for the casualty loss of household articles destroyed in the earthquake as well as a special tax treatment for losses to business assets in the damaged areas. As such, it was expected that many taxpayers would contact the NTA about their tax filings and payment, especially at the tax offices in damaged areas. To manage the demand, the NTA undertook the following measures:

- Dispatched additional officials to support the tax offices located in the damaged areas. For example, approximately 90 additional officials were sent to Ishinomaki tax office, a relatively large tax office in the damaged areas, where 50 officials are normally assigned. The officials were dispatched from nearby tax offices and regional tax bureaus. In total, 18 268 officials from other tax offices and 4 112 officials from regional tax bureaus across the country were dispatched by the end of December 2011.
- A satellite office was opened in Tokyo in order to mitigate the congestion at the telephone consultation centre. New special telephone numbers were installed to assist with the inquiries related to the disaster.
- Publicised and notified advice through brochures and the NTA website.
- Educational sessions and on-site consultations were arranged in co-operation with local authorities and relevant non-governmental organisations.

Anticipating demand after the earthquake

It was expected that many taxpayers would come to local tax offices, especially during the income tax filing season from February through March in the following year (2012). Therefore, the NTA supported tax offices in damaged areas in order to provide smooth services for taxpayers who suffered from the disaster. NTA sent 140 officials per day on average to tax offices in damaged areas from regional tax bureaus in metropolitan areas, as well as opened the satellite office for telephone consultation in the western part of Japan.

Lessons learnt

In addition to the measures implemented to support the disaster, NTA is also working on improving its capability to respond to future disasters, by revising the manual for disasters, based on the experience of the earthquake and by maintaining necessary supplies and equipment.

Ireland (Revenue) – eStamping Project

Background

In 2006 the eStamping Project was formed with the core purpose of addressing the fundamental business requirement of simplifying and modernising Stamp Duty processes for all stakeholders to better manage the demand generated in terms of contacts and documentation handling as a result of those existing processes.

These processes were modernised by the migration of the Stamp Duty Administration System (SDAS) onto the Integrated Taxation Services (ITS) architecture. Simplification was achieved by enabling taxpayers to file and pay Stamp Duty on line through

Revenue's secure Online Service - (ROS) - a self-service, self-assessment process with little or no intervention by Revenue staff.

Practices and procedures were analysed and overhauled and the processes whereby pre-stamping assurance checks were carried out were removed. The removal of these pre-assurance checks reduced processing times and thereby the time and cost burden for both Revenue and taxpayers. The assurance checks are now carried out post-stamping (and payment of duty), on a risk-assessed basis.

The new system came into effect on 31 December 2009 and has provided significant savings in terms of monetary and staff costs, increased internal efficiencies, improved customer service and processing times, augmented Revenue risk profiling and further enhances Revenue's reputation.

What was the problem?

There were many issues that needed to be addressed, including:

- a requirement to reduce counter and postal Stamp Duty contacts in order to release staff to perform other audit / compliance duties;
- a need to migrate customers to Self Service channels and, in particular, the online solution through Revenue Online Services (ROS);
- the existing Stamp Duty Administration System (SDAS) was costing Revenue approximately EUR 390 000 in maintenance costs in 2009 and it was anticipated that maintenance costs would be in the region of EUR 670 000 annually thereafter;
- the need and benefits from migrating the existing SDAS to the integrated ITS architecture was essential in terms of securing cost savings and enhancing efficiency. The inclusion of Stamp Duty in ITS would facilitate customer risk profiling to be carried out and reduce the risk of fraud while also streamlining financial processing;
- the need to advance and extend the use of new technology for Revenue's business in line with organisational policy;
- quicker turnaround times for eStamping Customers' refunds and consistency in eStamping refund processing were required;
- the requirement for improved accuracy of claim data;
- the need to reduce the volumes of paper records retained for stamp duty processing and refunds and storage thereof;
- the need to reduce printing costs.

How was it identified?

The ongoing high maintenance costs of the existing system, management of large staff numbers needed to administer the tax at a time when these numbers were reducing in other areas and the need to migrate staff to areas of compliance, debt management and collection were all evident.

In addition, large volumes of customer contacts were being managed through public offices, phone and written contacts. At the time of the property boom in Ireland the sheer volume of property transactions led to increased numbers of legal instruments and their accompanying payments being processed. This resulted in large backlogs of documentation and refund payments that, in turn, led to additional contacts and additional costs in administering these through use of overtime payments.

Revenue playing its part in the wider government reform agenda

This project also afforded opportunities for Revenue to improve its position on government-wide initiatives and programmes such as:

- to strategically position Revenue to incorporate Stamp Duty into an overall eConveyancing environment in the future;
- opportunity for the Property Registration Authority (PRA) to leverage an integrated validation check prior to accepting a registration claim, thereby increasing the overall assurance in the government-wide process;
- assistance in establishing a nationwide residential property sales register by the Property Services Regulatory Authority (PSRA).

How did Revenue go about developing responses and solution to deliver on the modernisation agenda?

The eStamping Project was an information technology solution to enable customers, predominantly solicitors, to comply with their obligations to file a Stamp Duty return and pay the appropriate liability. This facility supported the revised legislative changes that were enacted for the administration of Stamp Duty and is an online service available via ROS for taxpayers to file stamp duty returns (with a very limited option to file a paper-based return for input via Integrated Taxation Processing by Revenue staff). The solution also supports the arrangements for data sharing between Revenue and the Property Registration Authority and other state agencies such as the Central Statistics Office and the Valuation Office.

What options were considered?

Other options considered included:

- utilising the existing system and expanding its capacity to facilitate eStamping transactions through Revenue's existing online system – ROS;
- researching options used by IRAS (Singapore) and an off-the-shelf product solution, which could have been bought and maintained by that third-party provider.

What governance mechanisms were in place?

With the approval of the Revenue Board, and approved through Revenue's Management Advisory Committee (MAC), the project was set up with staff drawn from the Dublin Stamp Duty office utilising business expertise and experience to drive and deliver business and functional requirements for the system build. A Steering Group was also established which reported to a Project Board.

Project Board reports and updates were provided to the Information Technology Executive (ITEX), which had responsibility for the building of the information technology application.

The project utilised the Revenue Delivery Methodology (RDM), which was managed by the Project Management Office (PMO). The PMO had responsibility for ensuring that all elements of the build, test and implementation of the system were managed in accordance with the Project Plan, which had specific milestones, deadlines, resource metrics and deliverables.

Throughout the lifecycle of the project, a series of decision points arose where ITEX approval was required. These are summarised as follows:

- approval of a ***Project Origination Document*** (POD), which provides a summary of the business case and scope of the proposed project as well as a broad indication of likely costs;
- approval of a ***Project Initiation Document*** (PID), which provides an enhanced estimate of scope and cost but which also outlines details of the project timelines, control mechanisms, keys risks, stakeholder impacts, etc;
- approval of a ***Project Confirmation Document*** (PCD), which provides a refined set of project budgets which are developed following the completion of the appropriate requirements definition phase.

The initial PID document, therefore, was the final governance gateway, which provided ITEX with an overall project plan, supported by detailed project plans for every project team for the duration of the project and detailed cost estimates. The plan and estimates were based on the signed-off functional requirements and, as such, formed the basis for the allocation of the project budget by ITEX to initiate project development and business activities. The information provided in that document enabled ITEX to make the following decisions:

- approval of the project delivery timelines;
- approval of the total budget to be allocated, given that the initial figures estimated in the PID were broad estimates which were subsequently refined based on the signed-off functional requirements ; and
- approval of the project plans for each ICT&L and Business team.

The PID document also detailed the governance roles established for the life of the project.

What was the outcome?

Project results

E-Stamping allows solicitors and other practitioners to use ROS to file a stamp duty return, pay stamp duty and receive an electronic stamp duty certificate on-line.

The new e-Stamping system was launched successfully on 30 December 2009. Immediately after the launch of the new system approximately 73% of stamp duty returns were being made on line. At the beginning of March 2010, approximately 83% of stamp duty returns were being lodged on-line. This result far exceeded the original target of 30% for that period. At present, 99% of all returns are filed on-line.

Revenue believe that the success of the project can be attributed to the excellent design and implementation of the system in conjunction with an effective communications strategy, which succeeded in selling the new system to the target audience and convincing them of the advantages of using the on-line system over the paper equivalent.

Revenue's main focus now is on post stamping compliance and assurance checking.

Channel management

Public offices

From 22 December 2009 the main Stamp Duty public office in Dublin was closed to personal callers. By the end of 2010, the non-public regional stamp duty offices had also closed and customer services were centralised in Dublin on a back-office basis.

Mandatory e-filing

At the end of the second quarter of 2011, it became mandatory to file and pay stamp duty on line.

Since July 2012, the remaining pre-stamping assessment service was withdrawn by Revenue and Stamp Duty is now fully self-assessed in line with the governance and processes of all other self-assessed taxes.

Cost and benefits

The cost of the e-stamping project was estimated originally at EUR 6 million (EUR 5.998 million). The calculations of actual cost indicated that it closed at budget (EUR 5.950 million).

The main benefits of the new system include:

- the availability to customers of an efficient on-line stamping system, in accordance with our strategy on extending the use of ROS and developing more e-government services;
- the immediate addition of up-to-date stamping data to Revenue's information warehouse assisting more effective and efficient compliance work;
- elimination of the on-going high maintenance costs of the previous system – SDAS;
- closure of offices and reduction of contacts enabled staff to be redeployed for other essential audit/compliance work;
- inclusion of Stamp Duty Transactions in customer risk profiling and thereby reducing the risk of fraud;
- other significant internal cost savings for Revenue, including staff savings, printing costs, paper and storage of hard copy records, etc.

Taking into account staff savings and the savings on running the old stamping information technology system, Revenue estimate that the project will pay for itself in less than 3.5 years.

Lessons learnt

Communication strategy

It is essential to have a comprehensive and multi-faceted communication strategy to address all stakeholders – both internally for staff and externally for customers.

Our internal strategy focused on changes to existing practices in terms of administration and audit. This included regular updates on project progress to all staff, newsletters, operational instructions circulated to all staff including those involved in audit, and training for staff directly involved in the revised practices and procedures of the new system and its operation.

Our external strategy identified the various segments of our target audience and evolved specialised campaigns and messages for each segment. This ensured a clear and specific message was sent to enable full understanding of the opportunities and obligations for all those involved.

Early engagement with our target audiences encouraged meaningful contributions to assist with the successful design and smooth implementation of the new system and also enhanced relationships with certain representative groups. No major issues or difficulties presented themselves and any issues that arose were managed satisfactorily and with minimum impact on design or build.

Revenue provided extensive post-launch support, which included talks and seminars, visits to the larger users, comprehensive and updated information on the new system on Revenue's website and an expanded toll-free phone service for tax practitioners. In addition, Revenue continued to meet with the Law Society, on a monthly basis, to obtain feedback from users and to ensure that the new system is functioning well.

System build

During the actual research, analysis, description and agreement phase of the various functional design components of the system, it was essential that the business expertise was aligned with information technology knowledge so that the business requirements were clearly understood and that nothing was 'lost in translation'. This was a crucial element to ensuring that the final system built met the requirements of the business area. Misunderstanding of requirements could lead to additional costs resulting in changes or alternations to the design or scope of the build.

Consequently, at the initial planning stage, it was essential to be as thorough and detailed as possible when describing the tasks and each and every step needed to be undertaken for each and every stage of the build. It was also essential to provide as accurate a costing as possible for each step of each task in order to avoid underestimation of overall project costs.

New Zealand (NZ) Inland Revenue (IR) - Achieving channel shift

What was the problem?

- Customer contacts of a high volume, low value nature were exponentially increasing and forecasted to continue to grow.
- Difficulty servicing customer contacts through traditional phone service within reasonable timeframes; insufficient staff to meet demand, difficulty in re-routing calls to available capacity, significant call abandonment rates, etc.

- Increasing personnel and operating costs of printing/paper output (outward correspondence, forms, information, return, guides), in a time with increasing demand from government to 'do more with less'.
- *www.ird.govt.nz* provided a one-way electronic communication channel with customers (web-informed), where the customer had to print out the form, complete it and return it to IR.

How was it identified?

Key drivers which influenced IR's decision to embark on shifting customer demand from physical, paper and voice channels to self-service (eServices Programme) were:

- modernisation of business practices – other organisations both in NZ and overseas were moving to 'e' (electronic) as a way of cutting costs and modernising their businesses. IR needed to also move with these times or risk being left behind;
- increasingly expensive to use physical, paper and phone channels;
- customer demand for electronic services was being driven by increasing level of services being provided by other organisations;
- unacceptable wait times on the phone and delays in issuing paper output;
- reputational risk of not moving towards e-services;
- environmental change.

How did IR go about developing a response/solution to the problem?

IR took a building block approach to achieving a sustainable channel shift.

- The first step was to develop a Channel Shift Strategy. The strategy called out the following channels: website, online service, phone and business to business (known as B2B) and the emerging mobile channel.
- The IBM retail cross-channel maturity model was adapted to suit the IR environment, which articulates how change is achieved through a series of steps. In the NZ context, this would mean being able to turn off the paper that was issued (for example statement, notices, letters, forms, etc) and eliminate or reduce phone calls to the contact centre.
- Once the direction was clear, new initiatives were identified that would progressively increase IR's e-Channel maturity, enterprise architecture and organisational capability. IR was also able to leverage the introduction of significant social policy changes (for example Working for Families, KiwiSaver and Student Loans) as a means to progressing its e-services.
- Throughout, the enterprise view has been one of re-usability and scalability. Any new service or system needed to be developed so that it was easily extended, connected into or duplicated as additional needs were identified.

What governance mechanisms were in place?

- The eServices Programme was established in 2009 and charged with delivering trusted self-service channels for IR, its partners and customers. Operating as a Programme allowed for dedicated resourcing to be assigned to focus on identifying the best opportunities to increase IR's maturity in the design and delivery of e-services.

- The eServices Programme is overseen by a Programme Sponsor (Tier 3 IR Manager) and Programme Board comprised of Tier 3 and 4 IR Managers.
- The Programme Office is responsible for the day to day management of the programme, driving strategy (on behalf of the Board) and business change, and ensuring uptake of the new services are maximised in conjunction with the wider IR business.
- There are three workstreams, each responsible for a number of specific projects and initiatives set up to deliver agreed outputs. Each of the initiatives are led on a day to day basis by a Workstream Manager or a Project Manager. The work is delivered on behalf of a Project Sponsor (by a 4th tier manager from the key IR business group) who in turn reports to the Board. Workstream Advisory Groups guide progress of the initiatives and make recommendations to the Board as to appropriate design and development requirements.
- In addition, the Programme Board is overseen by a Project Governance Investment Committee comprising senior managers from across key IR business groups (Service Delivery, IT, Finance, HR, Corporate Risk & Assurance, Policy Advice).
- All projects use the IR change process and apply it using the fit for purpose approach. All projects have to have a:
  - statement of work detailing the business case associated with the system and process changes required;
  - design Completion report documenting technical and non-technical specifications of change and final costs;
  - implementation Readiness report documenting preparedness of the business to go live with change.
- In addition to this, the role of the Business Change Owner (who are board members) is instrumental to ensuring that benefits are delivered in the business as a result of the changes that the projects are delivering.

What was the outcome?

Successfully delivered over 20 projects and initiatives to improve the uptake of eChannel Services and USD 2.9 million of gross benefits.

- Online Services customers have increased from 340 000 in 2009-10 to 1 033 000 of in June 2012.
- Since April 2011, almost 1 500 tax agents have moved to the B2B Tax Agent Web Service.
- IR assisted contacts have decreased from around 9 million in 2009-10 to less than 6 million in 2010-11.
- With the introduction of the new Voice ID services in November 2011, IR is now the biggest voice biometric installation in NZ and uptake rates are at least as high

as similar organisations in Australia. As of June 2012 our enrolments had reached 250 000.

- IR's first Mobile Web Application was launched in May 2012 with the aim of improving the experience for those users accessing the IR website via mobile devices, smart phones and tablets. Research indicated that there were 50 000 visits per year, and without any communication activity (due to start in July) the application was averaging between 200-300 visits per day.

Lessons learnt

- IR's earlier approach of 'build it and they will come' did not result in the uptake that had been expected. IR learnt that a strategic approach (with the buy-in and support across the entire organisation) was needed to achieve the desired uptake of self services. Once the strategic direction was agreed, specific projects were then identified and deliberately undertaken to achieve the channel shift.
- If one of the organisational drivers for increasing e-uptake is to reduce costs, then it is important to have transparency of all costs involved in the design, delivery and support of the service, across all relevant business groups and at all levels of the organisation.
- Moving into 'e' requires the development of new capabilities which small countries like NZ have a skill shortage in. Often the architecture required for the operation of 'e' does not already exist within the organisation and will need to be built alongside existing systems.

Inland Revenue Authority of Singapore (IRAS) – Demand management strategies

Background

Customer Relationship Framework

IRAS has a Customer Relationship Framework (see Figure 5.1) which is a guide to managing taxpayer relationships and feedback and improving customer satisfaction. The framework consists of elements which are related to demand management because proactive management of taxpayers' need for service and information is essential to achieving customer satisfaction. These elements are:

- desired IRAS experience;
- proactive customer relationship management – 'No need for service is the best service';
- channel management – By encouraging self-help;
- timely & accurate information and easy & convenient services;
- contact information analysis.

Desired IRAS experience

Underpinning the Customer Relationship Framework is the 'Desired IRAS Experience' which articulates how the IRAS wants to take its relationship with taxpayers to the next level by not only addressing the physical needs of its taxpayers (for example, information and services) but to also consider their emotional needs as well. To achieve this, IRAS has articulated different desired service outcomes for each customer group:

- voluntary compliant taxpayers who do not contact IRAS;
- voluntary compliant taxpayers who have contact with IRAS;
- unaware and negligent taxpayers;
- errant taxpayers.

IRAS calibrates and differentiates its approaches and programmes according to the compliance profiles of taxpayers so as to create the right incentives for taxpayers to be compliant. Compliant taxpayers will be encouraged to self-help because IRAS provides easy, convenient and reliable e-services.

Figure 5.1. Customer Relationship Framework

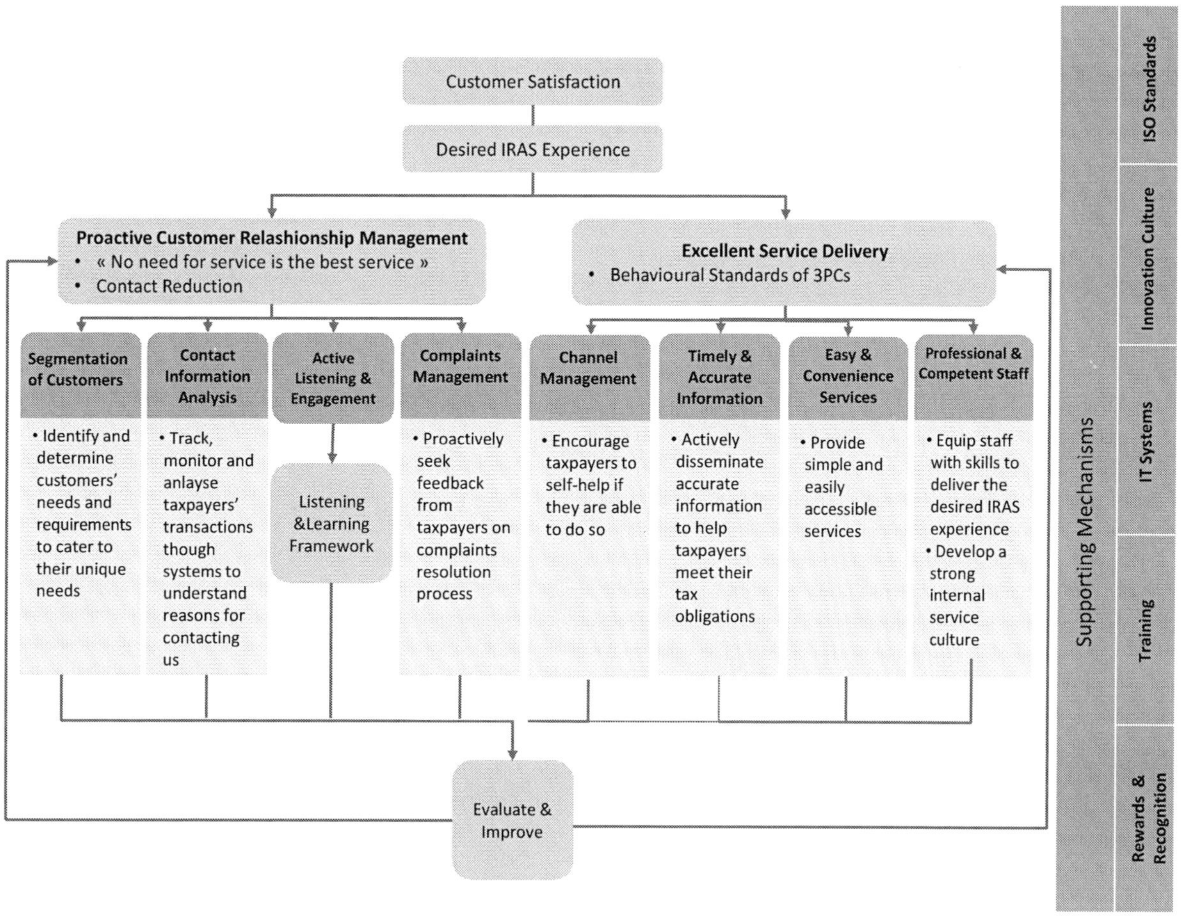

Source: Inland Revenue Authority of Singapore

Service strategy

IRAS strives to make rules, systems and processes so simple and clear that taxpayers would not need any service from IRAS as the IRAS believes in '*No need for service is the best service*'. Where this is not possible, IRAS encourages taxpayers to self-help. If taxpayers need assisted services, IRAS prefers the taxpayer to call, followed by an e-mail, then write and lastly to come in and see IRAS. IRAS sets service standards to influence taxpayers' behaviour shift towards the preferred channels, as depicted in Figure 5.2.

Figure 5.2. Service strategy and service standards

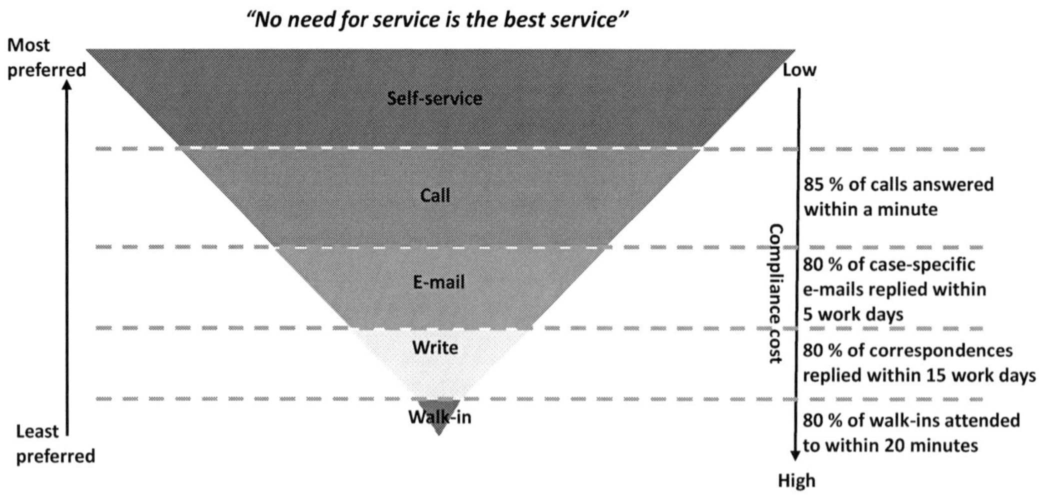

Source: Inland Revenue Authority of Singapore

Contact information analysis

IRAS actively tracks, monitors and analyses taxpayer contacts. Action plans are developed to address causes of demand and reduce taxpayers' need for service.

A review cycle includes the following steps:

- collect statistics of the various modes of contact through the system or via manual tracking;
- for areas where IRAS wants to target efforts in reducing demand such as walk-ins, conduct surveys to further understand why taxpayers contact IRAS;
- review contacts received to identify the most common nature of enquiries and their causes;
- where necessary, conduct focus groups and meetings with frontline staff to gain in-depth understanding of the root causes of demand;
- identify enhancements to address the reasons for contacts;
- implement changes for the following year.

Examples of demand management solutions/responses

IRAS has implemented a number of initiatives to reduce contacts which include the following.

Filetax 2-way SMS

From yearly review cycles, IRAS observed that taxpayers often contact during the filing period to check if they need to file a return. Therefore, IRAS not only launched an online service for taxpayers to check if they need to file but also a two-way SMS service so that taxpayers without internet access can check their filing status on-the-go.

Return my call service

To better manage demand for assisted phone services during the filing period, IRAS introduced the Return My Call Service. With this service, taxpayers can send an SMS to request for a call back from IRAS instead of calling the help lines and waiting on the line. 92% of users rated this service as very good.

E-file early SMS reminders

Reminder SMS are sent to taxpayers who have not filed in the current year or who filed late in the previous year. This serves to:

- reduce contacts during the filing period as taxpayers would not need to contact the IRAS to check if they are required to file;
- reduce downstream contacts in response to enforcement actions after the filing deadline.

Collaboration with government agencies

Taxpayers often contact IRAS to obtain three back-year copies of their tax bills for submission to the Immigration & Checkpoints Authority (ICA) along with their applications for citizenship and permanent residency. IRAS first introduced an e-service so that taxpayers can access back-year tax bills on line and were able to print them. Then IRAS took a further step to link up with the ICA so that the information can be provided directly to ICA so long as authorisation has been provided by the taxpayer. The taxpayer now no longer needs to access and print their tax bills from our system for submission.

Simplification of administrative procedures and tax laws

Besides encouraging self-help and targeting causes of demand, IRAS continuously simplify tax administration and laws for individuals, businesses and property owners. Simplification will lead to a reduction in contacts.

IRAS does not restrict itself to simplification of administrative procedures only. As IRAS interacts with taxpayers directly, it receives a lot of taxpayer feedback including the compliance cost incurred by them. Hence IRAS plays an important role in tax policy review and does make proposals on simplifications of the tax law. Following are some examples.

- Administrative procedures
  - *Simplified Filing for Small Companies* - From 2012, small companies with an annual revenue of USD 1 million or below may file a shortened three-page Income Tax Return instead of a seven-page tax return. About 70% of companies are expected to benefit from this initiative and this is likely to reduce the contacts from these companies or tax agents.
  - *Simplified Interactive Voice Response Call Flows* - Through a survey done with taxpayers, IRAS noticed that taxpayers were not satisfied with the current design of the Interactive Voice Response (IVR) call flows. The taxpayers considered the IVR a hindrance to their ultimate goal of speaking directly with an officer and also felt that the IVR had too many steps. To address this feedback and minimise

repeated attempts by taxpayers to reach an officer, the IVR call flows were simplified. IRAS capped the time taken, from the time the call is connected to the time when the 'speak to officer' option is announced at below 45 seconds by providing only 1 level of menu and a maximum of 6 IVR options. IRAS further increased usability by removing IVR options with low usage and placing the high usage ones upfront.

– *Proactive Adjustment of Provisional Instalment Plans* - IRAS allows taxpayers to pay their taxes via a 12 monthly instalment cycle starting in May, after the filing deadline, based on a provisional amount. The provisional amount is normally based on the past year's instalment. IRAS noticed contacts from taxpayers who were unhappy or confused that IRAS continued to deduct the same amount even though there was drastic reduction in income. To reduce such contacts, IRAS accelerated the assessments of taxpayers with drastic reduction in income so that their monthly payments reflect the current year's tax liability accurately.

- Tax laws
  – *Non-taxation of the Net Annual Value of Residential Properties and Alimony* - Arising from taxpayer feedback, IRAS proposed to tax-exempt net annual value of residential properties and alimony which were accepted by the Finance Ministry. This makes it easier for affected taxpayers to understand their tax obligations and minimises their need for assisted services.

Governance mechanisms & outcomes

Governance structure

IRAS' organisation structure, which is based on the major tax types allows it to deliver taxpayer-centric services. The Tax Management Division drives taxpayer compliance, through the delivery of customised services to the specific taxpayer segments. These divisions are also responsible for driving the service-related Key Performance Indicators, including demand management, which are monitored at an organisational level.

Key performance indicators

- Number of frontline contacts.
- Number of frontline contacts per taxpayer.
- Percentage of contacts by self-help.
- Adoption rate of key e-services.
- Taxpayer overall satisfaction index.

Outcome

- Over the five year period from 2007 to 2011, the overall number of contacts and number of frontline contacts per taxpayer have been decreasing (see Figures 5.3 and 5.4). In addition, there has been an overall increase in the percentage of contacts through the self-help channel which is a positive sign that IRAS is moving taxpayers away from assisted services (see Figure 5.5).

Figure 5.3. Volume of contacts received (2007 to 2011 fiscal year)

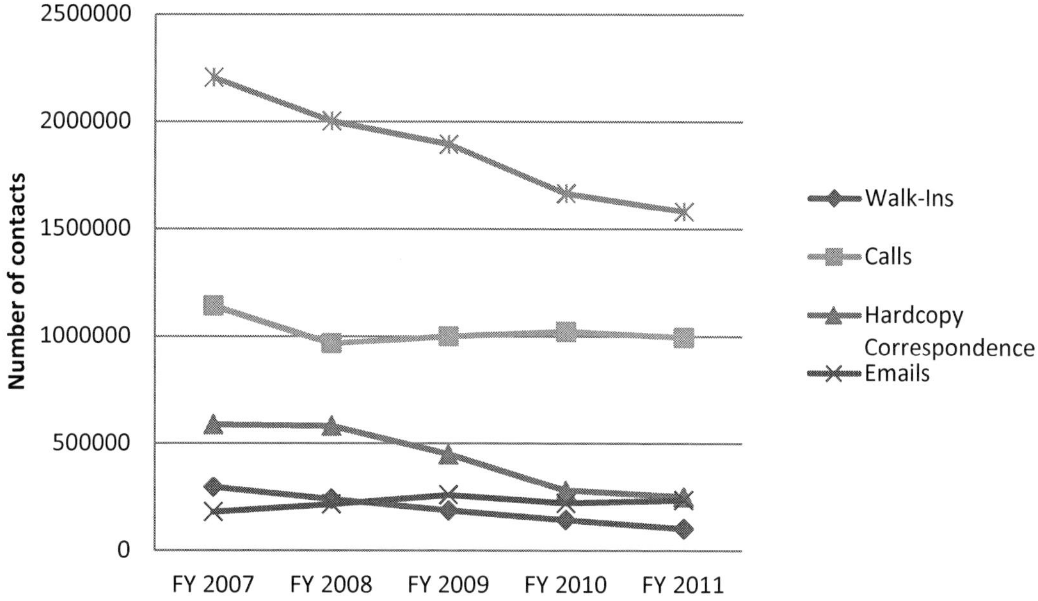

Source: Inland Revenue Authority of Singapore

Figure 5.4. Number of frontline contacts per taxpayer (2009 to 2011 fiscal year)

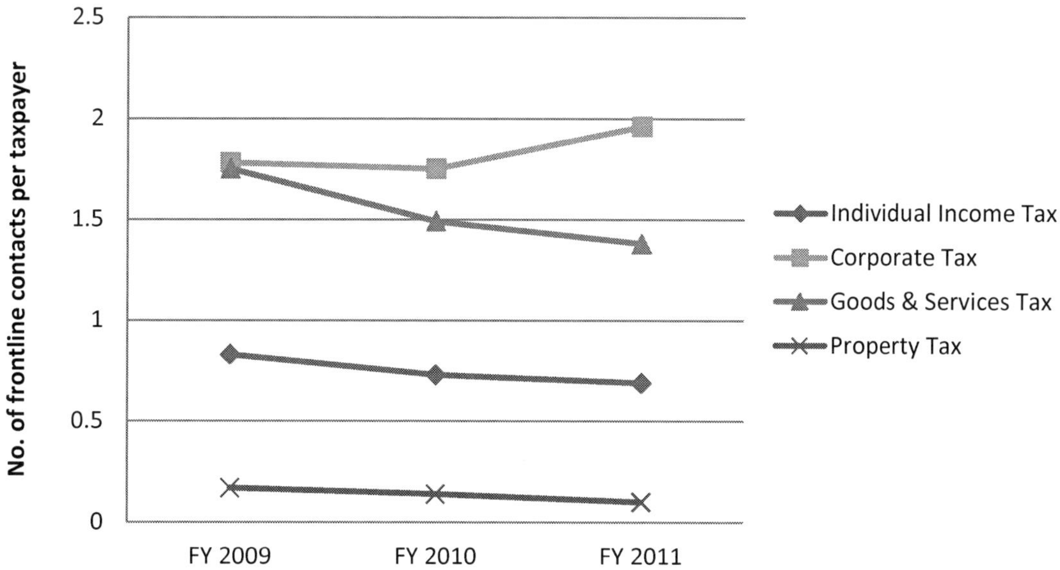

Source: Inland Revenue Authority of Singapore

Figure 5.5. Percentage of contacts by self-help (2009 to 2011 fiscal year)

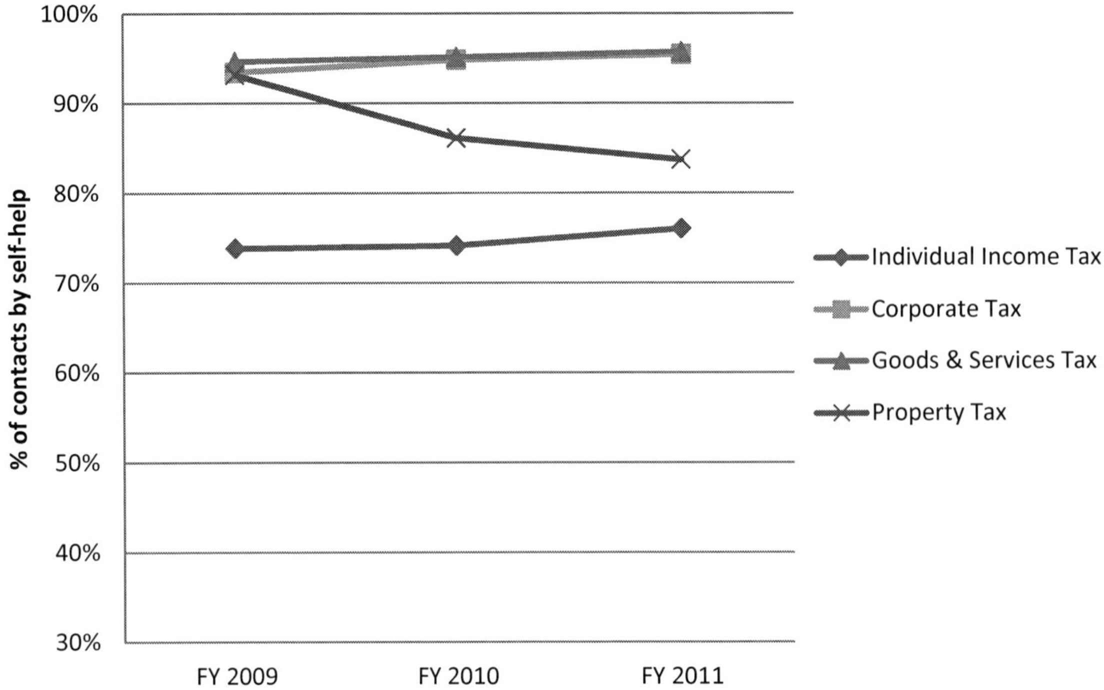

Source: Inland Revenue Authority of Singapore

- About 1 million individual income taxpayers file their returns every year. Over the last three years the e-filing rate continues to increase while contact rate continues to fall (see Figure 5.6).

Figure 5.6. Trends in e-filing and contact rates

Source: Inland Revenue Authority of Singapore

- Positive results from the Taxpayer Survey 2011
  - 94.7% of taxpayers are satisfied or very satisfied with IRAS' level of service.
  - 13.5% of taxpayers are advocates for IRAS and are very willing to say positive things about their experience with IRAS.

United Kingdom - Demand management in Her Majesty's Revenue and Customs (HMRC)

What was the problem?

HMRC runs 16 contact centres, with approximately 6 000 staff handling around 60 million telephone calls a year. HMRC has to deal with peaks and troughs in demand, primarily driven by statutory deadlines. This can lead to fluctuating levels of performance in terms of call attempts handled. To put this in perspective, over the course of the year from April 2010 to March 2011, HMRC handled 48% of call attempts against an industry standard of 90%.

The Demand Management programme was born in response to this. The goal of the programme is to:

- eliminate low value calls;
- re-engineer processes and improve forms and guidance so customers don't need to contact HMRC;
- migrate customers to self-serve options.

The programme is a key enabler for the departmental goal of reaching 90% call attempts handled.

How was it identified and how did HMRC develop a response/solution to the problem?

HMRC uses call classification data to identify problem areas. This data is derived from the 'voice of the customer'. Specially trained contact centre advisers classify calls based on the customer's initial query. The data is collated weekly for analysis by teams within the Demand Management programme and used:

- to drive discussion amongst front line advisers and encourage suggestions for tackling specific contact types. These are turned into detailed solutions through 'deep dives' such as focused research and problem solving techniques;
- to inform the development of automated messaging on HMRC's help lines and Frequently Asked Questions on the website;
- to inform policy and process owners about what is driving contact in their areas – and make them accountable for developing demand reduction solutions alongside the Demand Management programme;
- to develop propositions for enhancing our digital (self-serve) options for customers.

Options considered?

HMRC does not adopt a 'one size fits all' approach. Instead, interventions are tailored through a detailed understanding of what is driving customers to call. For instance, where call classification data showed that the main reason customers phoned was because they didn't understand a certain letter, the programme worked across HMRC to make changes to that letter. Interventions include:

- Changes to web pages to ensure these answer common customer questions.
- Changes to wording on letters or forms to make it easier for customers to understand what, if anything, they need to do.
- Development of automated messages to answer specific customer questions, for example 'what is my Tax Credit payment date after a public holiday'?
- Changes to call scripts so that these fit with the online offering. For instance, where HMRC have a detailed online calculator that customers can use to check their eligibility for certain benefits, advisers simply ask whether customers have used this service rather than repeating the process in all cases.
- Changes to business processes to cut out steps that lead to low value customer contact.
- Provision of online 'Where's my reply?' tools, where some customers can check standard response times before ringing to chase progress.

HMRC is also investing in voice recognition technology.

Governance mechanisms

The Demand Management programme has a range of interventions, from small-scale projects looking at making changes to individual letters, to much larger projects requiring major investment in information technology changes.

Governance mechanisms differ depending on the scale of the project. All projects are required to submit a business case and benefits forecast setting out the likely scale of call reduction. The business cases for projects requiring investment are clearly more comprehensive and subject to a higher level of clearance depending on the size of investment required. Business cases for multi-million pound investments are cleared through HMRC's top level investment committee and then through the Cabinet Office.

A notable success of the programme has been to gain funding for a portfolio of changes to take place outside its direct control. Parts of HMRC who identify products or processes that drive high volumes of contact can access funding from the programme. They can use this to make changes to reduce demand.

Top-level governance of the Demand Management Programme is achieved through the Demand Management Programme Board. This is chaired by the Director for Change within Personal Tax, who is also the Senior Responsible Officer for the Programme. Senior representatives from all business areas with an interest in Demand Management sit on the board. This includes the Head of HMRC's Contact Centres, the Director for Customer and Strategy within Personal Tax and the Process Owners for Benefits and Credits, Personal Tax and Business tax. Top-level representation on the Programme Board ensures that Demand Management remains a key priority for business areas.

There is a number of working level groups that sit below the Programme Board to support it. In advance of the monthly Programme Board meetings, there are monthly bi-lateral meetings to discuss performance with representatives from each of the lines of business. There are also monthly joint working groups composed of representatives from the programme and from the line of business. These groups look at interventions in detail.

The overall aim of the governance arrangements is to ensure that Business Areas responsible for demand are involved at all levels in interventions to reduce it.

Were the intended outcomes delivered?

Yes. The programme has a target to reduce calls to contact centre advisers by 27.8 million by March 2015. In the first year, it reduced calls to advisers by 10.7 million. This achievement contributed to an increase in call attempts handled from 48% in 2010-11 to 74.4% in 2011-12.

Lessons learnt

'Join up'. Allocate accountability to the parts of your organisation that are generating the demand. The Demand Management programme really gained momentum once the parts of HMRC whose products or processes were generating demand took on accountability for this and worked in joint teams with the programme to identify and implement solutions.

'Senior commitment'. Although this accountability is exercised at project level – the impetus came from the very top – HMRC's Executive Committee who instructed Directors General that they were accountable for the downstream demand of their processes. This is reflected in the Demand Management Programme Board where Process owner representatives, who are not part of the programme, each give an update on progress to reduce demand in their area. This meeting is chaired at Director level, which helps to focus attention on the issues.

Bibliography

Australian Taxation Office, Australia, *www.ato.gov.au/*

Japan National Tax Agency (NTA), Japan, *www.nta.go.jp/foreign_language/*

Revenue, Ireland, *www.revenue.ie/en/index.html*

New Zealand (NZ) Inland Revenue (IR), New Zealand, *www.ird.govt.nz/*

Inland Revenue Authority of Singapore, Singapore, *www.iras.gov.sg/irashome/default.aspx*

Her Majesty's Revenue and Customs, United Kingdom, *www.hmrc.gov.uk/*

Annex A

The following is an example of how the Australian Taxation Office (ATO) governs service delivery for its organisation at the strategic level:

Figure A.1. Model of committee structure

Source: Australian Taxation Service

Table A.1. Strategic Services Committee

Committee Name	ATO Service Improvement Steering Committee (SISC)
Chair	Second Commissioner (Operations and Enterprise Solutions & Technology)
Members (8)	Channel Representatives at National Programme Manager level Chief Operating Officer, and Senior Business Representatives
Frequency	At least on a monthly basis.
Reporting	The Committee reports to the ATO Executive biannually
Role	The SISC reports to the ATO Executive Committee on ATO service strategy progress, outcomes, risks and issues, providing assurance that ATO service improvement has appropriate strategic level corporate governance. The SISC makes recommendations to the ATO Executive Committee on the ATO's strategic direction and implementation for ATO service improvement. The SISC supports business areas with high level guidance and direction on agreed enterprise service improvement strategic direction, principles and approach. The SISC will sponsor senior executive corporate design meetings. The SISC is supported by a sub-committee whose membership is at the Assistant Commissioner level. The chair of the sub-committee attends SISC meetings as an observer. The sub-committee reports to the SISC on a quarterly basis. For service improvement initiatives with an information technology dependency, the committee will work with the information technology executive to provide guidance on priority of information technology investments, ensuring the integrity of the enterprise solution and alignment with the broader change agenda.
Responsibilities	Ensure service improvement aligns with the ATO strategic direction, principles and design standards. Ensure appropriate corporate governance mechanisms are applied to the service improvement agenda and it is managed at an enterprise level. Ensure a co-ordinated approach to service improvement across the ATO. Be alert to potential opportunities in both the internal and external environments. Ensure service outcomes and experiences meet stakeholder expectations. Give full effect to whole-of-government strategic direction. Ensure the ATO maintains a reputation of being a leader in the implementation of large change programmes.

The following is an example of how the Australian Taxation Office (ATO) is governing from an operational perspective service delivery for its organisation:

Table A.2. Operational Services Committee

Committee Name	ATO Service Improvement Sub Committee
Chair	Assistant Commissioner, Strategic Programme, Operations
Members (Business Line representatives)	Assistant Commissioners Strategic Programme, Operations Support & Capability (Chair) Co-ordination Delivery, Customer Service & Solutions Strategic Communications, Corporate Relations Corporate Governance, Corporate Relations Publishing, Corporate Relations Online & Access Design, Business Solutions Practitioners & Consultation, Tax Practitioners and Lodgement Service Work Management, Client Account Services Services & Assistance, Micro Enterprises and Individuals
Frequency	At least on a monthly basis.
Reporting	The Service Improvement Steering Committee is to be briefed by the chair on a quarterly basis. Stakeholders are to be informed of key decisions through appropriate mechanisms on a regular basis.
Role	Under the framework set by the Service Improvement Steering Committee, the Service Improvement Sub Committee provides advice, input and support to the Service Improvement Steering Committee to assist it in its role of establishing and steering the ATO's strategic service delivery direction. The terms of reference of the Sub Committee have been derived from, and are aligned to, the terms of reference of the Service Improvement Steering Committee. The Service Improvement Sub Committee will influence to ensure strategic alignment but will not interfere in sub-plan lines of management or work programmes beyond its purpose outlined in the terms of reference. The Sub Committee provides advice and guidance for existing structures through the chair, internal members and internal advisers.
Responsibilities	Contributing to the direction of the ATO channel strategy. Championing the ATO channel strategy` and an integrated, enterprise wide approach to service delivery. Providing design and directional oversight of key service delivery improvement initiatives and projects. Identifying and progressing opportunities to improve service delivery and the client experience. Understanding whole of government service delivery initiatives and considering ATO service delivery improvements in the whole of government context. Maximising opportunities to shift information, interactions and transactions to preferred service channels. Ensuring communications about ATO service delivery reflect the strategic direction of service improvement activities. Escalation of issues to the Service Improvement Steering Committee. Quarterly reporting to the Service Improvement Steering Committee.

ORGANISATION FOR ECONOMIC CO-OPERATION AND DEVELOPMENT

The OECD is a unique forum where governments work together to address the economic, social and environmental challenges of globalisation. The OECD is also at the forefront of efforts to understand and to help governments respond to new developments and concerns, such as corporate governance, the information economy and the challenges of an ageing population. The Organisation provides a setting where governments can compare policy experiences, seek answers to common problems, identify good practice and work to co-ordinate domestic and international policies.

The OECD member countries are: Australia, Austria, Belgium, Canada, Chile, the Czech Republic, Denmark, Estonia, Finland, France, Germany, Greece, Hungary, Iceland, Ireland, Israel, Italy, Japan, Korea, Luxembourg, Mexico, the Netherlands, New Zealand, Norway, Poland, Portugal, the Slovak Republic, Slovenia, Spain, Sweden, Switzerland, Turkey, the United Kingdom and the United States. The European Union takes part in the work of the OECD.

OECD Publishing disseminates widely the results of the Organisation's statistics gathering and research on economic, social and environmental issues, as well as the conventions, guidelines and standards agreed by its members.

OECD PUBLISHING, 2, rue André-Pascal, 75775 PARIS CEDEX 16
(23 2013 17 1 P) ISBN 978-92-64-20076-0 – No. 60691 2013-01